FALSE GUILT

Breaking the Tyranny of an Overactive Conscience

STEVE SHORES

NAVPRESS

BRINGING TRUTH TO LIFE

NavPress Publishing Group

P.O. Box 35001, Colorado Springs, Colorado 80935

The Navigators is an international Christian organization. Jesus Christ gave His followers the Great Commission to go and make disciples (Matthew 28:19). The aim of The Navigators is to help fulfill that commission by multiplying laborers for Christ in every nation.

NavPress is the publishing ministry of The Navigators. NavPress publications are tools to help Christians grow. Although publications alone cannot make disciples or change lives, they can help believers learn biblical discipleship, and apply what they learn to their lives and ministries.

Library of Congress Catalog Card Number: 93-39284
ISBN 08910-97627

Some of the anecdotal illustrations in this book are true to life and are included with the permission of the persons involved. All other illustrations are composites of real situations, and any resemblance to people living or dead is coincidental.

Unless otherwise identified, all Scripture quotations in this publication are taken from the *New American Standard Bible* (NASB), © The Lockman Foundation 1960, 1962, 1963, 1968, 1971, 1972, 1973, 1975, 1977.

Shores, Steve.
    False guilt : breaking the tyranny of an overactive conscience / Steve Shores
      p. cm.
    Includes bibliographical references.
    ISBN 0-89109-762-7
    1. Peace of mind. 2. Guilt—Religious aspects—Christianity. 3. Conscience—Religious aspects—Christianity. 4. Shame—Religious aspects—Christianity. 5. Christian life—1960- I. Title.
BV4908.5.S48   1993
241'.1—dc20   93-39284
                                     CIP

Printed in the United States of America

FOR A FREE CATALOG OF
NAVPRESS BOOKS & BIBLE STUDIES,
CALL 1-800-366-7788 (USA)
or 1-416-499-4615 (CANADA)

CONTENTS

▼ ▼

How Do You Know If You Have an Overactive Conscience?

MOST OF US Christians don't get it. We don't comprehend the fact that we are not on probation. Something really is over with, but we don't feel that way. We hear, "It is finished," but we live as if Christ said, "It is still up in the air." Many of us live *as if nothing decisive happened at the cross.*

We live as if we have to finish what Christ began. Proving that we are worth something becomes our focus rather than resting in having been forgiven and declared righteous as a free gift. We feel an uneasiness that tyrannizes us. We can't rest. We aren't doing enough. We are falling behind somehow. We need to pray more, witness more, go to more church meetings, have more devotional times, do more good works, more ministry. Where, in all this, is the peace that Christ talks about? When do we get to "punch out"?

Much of the energy behind our frenzied activity lies in our feeling vaguely unacceptable. We sense that we don't measure up, but we don't want anyone to find out. We are like someone sitting in an expensive restaurant with a forty-dollar entree in front of him, knowing that he has five dollars in his wallet. There is going to come, he knows, a moment of reckoning when his assets don't measure up to his obligations. There is our problem: We sense we owe far more than we can pay. We are terrified that our inadequacy will be dragged into the open for all to see. We fear any moment of reckoning that might come. We can, for example, see ourselves in the man or woman who wants to gain a level of success far beyond what he or she really needs. This drive is not rooted in material want but in the fear of being exposed as inadequate. This person tries desperately to add to the five dollars in his wallet, but somehow it all leaks away, and he begins each new day in the hole.

Ever feel like you're in the hole each morning? Ever feel as if you can never do enough? Your sense of duty won't let you rest? Your conscience nags you: "You call this acceptable? You think this is enough? Look at all you've not yet done! Look at all you have done that's not acceptable! Get going!" This badgering, pushy voice is that of an overactive conscience driven by false guilt.

You may not easily recognize this voice at first. Having an overactive conscience is not like having a cold. When you have a cold, you don't wonder whether you do or not. Your nose itches, you sneeze, you feel three thousand years old, and your head is full of concrete. An overactive conscience is a bit more subtle. There is no single manifestation of it that you can point to and say, "There it is!" It can be downright elusive. Maybe a description will help us get at it.

One man who struggled with an overactive conscience said that he "felt more like a human doing than a human being." His is a good portrayal of the *feeling* that comes with a conscience that is driven by false guilt. You feel weary but driven, stressed but used to it, on the treadmill but what else is there? There is little freedom, little spontaneity, and few times where pressure is truly gone. You feel as though you have never quite done enough, or that what you have done is never quite good enough. A feeling of falling short hangs over you like a bad reputation.

Three sets of questions, each with some explanation, follow. An affirmative answer to any or all of these questions may indicate that you struggle with false guilt and an overactive conscience.

Do you ever feel something like this: "Something is wrong with me. There is some stain on me, or something badly flawed that I can neither scrub out nor repair"? Does this feeling persist even though you have become a Christian? Do you ever feel that, though you're grateful that Christ has delivered you from the penalty of your sins, His work has somehow stopped short of real transformation?

The overactive conscience has no power to deliver us from either the fact or the feeling that something is wrong with us. In fact, the guilt-driven conscience increases the feeling that something is wrong with us, even for those who have become Christians. The *fact* that something is wrong with us is quite real and is addressed in the atoning work of Christ. If embracing what Christ has done for us doesn't take away the *feeling* that something is wrong with us, then that feeling is coming from elsewhere. The first three sections of this book address what that "elsewhere" might be and what is involved in it.

A second set of questions. Is Thanksgiving sort of a difficult time of year for you? Do you find it hard to muster up the Norman Rockwell spirit—you know . . . Mom and Dad and grandparents and kids all seated around mounds of food? Dad is carving the turkey with a sure and gentle expression on his face (somehow, he knows how to carve that thing into thin sheets instead of hunks that would challenge a Doberman), and everyone looks so, well, so thankful? Do you find yourself, at any time of the year, dutifully thanking or praising God without much passion? Is it tough for you genuinely to affirm the idea that this existence of ours is basically a joyful thing?

The overactive conscience has no power to infuse joy. It is a grim, mechanical, dutiful thing. It fills us with anxious sensitivity to "doing what is right." We struggle under the burden of campaigning for approval. Somehow, though, we never know whether we have enough votes. This uncertainty increases our anxiety and thus we try harder. The person with an overactive conscience knows no rest, only labor.

A third set of questions: How big is your dance floor? What I mean is, How much freedom do you have? Do you feel confined by Christianity? To you, is it mainly a set of restrictions? Is it primarily a source of limits: don't do this, and don't do that? Does your Christianity have more to do with walls than with windows? Is it a place of narrowness or a place where light and air and liberty pour in?

The person driven by false guilt is afraid of freedom because in every act of freedom is the possibility of offending someone. Offending someone is anathema! Other people are seen as pipelines of approval. If they're offended, the pipeline shuts down. There must be no offensiveness, ever. The person with an overactive conscience is thus willing to sacrifice freedom to keep the pipeline of approval open. It may be miserable to live a cramped and predictable life, but it feels far too risky to throw open the windows, put on some dance music, and expand your dance floor.

Does the "stain" of feeling something is vaguely but deeply wrong persist despite all scrubbing? Do you struggle with thanksgiving and praise to God, or does joy seem hard to come by? Are you confined and cornered in what you see as Christianity? False guilt, along with the overactive conscience that accompanies, is a hard master. Let's see if we can develop a way of thinking that might break its tiresome chains, dismantle its confining walls, and let light and air and liberty pour in.

PART ONE

WHAT IS
AN OVERACTIVE
CONSCIENCE?

CHAPTER ONE

Portraying
the Overactive Conscience

THE MISSION OF a person's overactive conscience is *to attract the expectations of others*. Imagine a bare light bulb outdoors on a summer night, relentlessly bombarded by the bugs that are attracted to its glare. This is a picture of an overactive conscience. It is a magnet for expectations. Others' expectations are the "bugs" that the overactive conscience intends to lure. Without those expectations, we have nothing to work with, no raw material for gaining approval. The more "bugs" the better!

By contrast, envision a light bulb burning inside a screened porch on a summer night. The bugs are still attracted, but they bounce off the screen. *The overactive conscience has no screen*. What's more, we don't *want* it to have a screen. Again, the more "bugs" or expectations attracted the better. Why? Because of what the overactive conscience motivates us to do. Its whole purpose is to meet expectations to gain approval and with that approval to fill an emptiness in the soul.

A key to understanding the overactive conscience is the word *active*. We have a conscience that is always on the go. False guilt makes us restless, continually looking for a rule to be kept, a scruple to observe, an expectation to be fulfilled, or a way to be an asset to a person or a group. The idea of being an asset is crucial to understanding the overactive conscience. When I am convinced that I am an asset, a "good" person, then life works pretty well. When I fear that I've let someone down, that I've been a liability, then life falls apart; and I must work hard to win my way back into the favor of others. I must attract and meet *more* expectations to regain my lost status.

The overactive conscience, then, is a magnet for expectations. These expectations can come from oneself, parents (whether alive or deceased), friends, bosses, peers, God, or distorted images of God. The point is that false guilt makes the overactive conscience voracious for expectations. Because of this, the overactive conscience sends out signals that tell others the person is open to expectations from them.

HOW THE OVERACTIVE CONSCIENCE SIGNALS FOR EXPECTATIONS

Physical and "Body Language" Signals

Some of these signals are physical. I may, for example, assume a submissive posture, evade eye contact, or develop a facial expression, all to communicate that I want to meet the expectations of those around me. Imagine for a moment that you meet someone, say at an office party, whose posture is slumped (the shoulders may be rounded and forward), whose eye movement is furtive and tentative so that eye contact is rare, and whose face gives an expression of appeal (eyebrows up, a very slight, rigid smile).

Whether you realize it or not, you are likely to relax around this person. But yours won't be the type of relaxing that comes when you're in the presence of healthy strength. It will be the kind of relaxing that comes when you realize you're superior, that the other person is weak, unlikely to "draw the sword." You realize you can get what you want with this person. You may find yourself moving into a conversation in which you are the center. You may begin telling stories about yourself that are faintly laudatory and fairly unusual for you to tell. Why? Because you are reading physical signals from another person that say, "Go ahead, use me for a screen. Project on me your thoughts about why you think you're worth something, especially if that makes you feel better." Body language, then, can signal a readiness to submit to the expectations of others.

Verbal Signals

Signals can also come through the verbal channel. For example, Brenda was a middle-aged Christian woman who almost invariably added the phrase "and stuff" on to statements she made in conversation. She might say, in response to a question about her prayer times, "Well, I just pray about all my friends and their needs and stuff." As we talked about why she used that phrase so readily, it emerged that she was nervous in expressing herself. She was afraid that any revealing of what was inside her would come under criticism. On the other hand, she wanted to engage with people to some degree; she didn't want to withdraw completely. To solve this dilemma, she began to pad her sentences with phrases that would communicate: "There's more, but I don't know if I can overcome my fear of expressing it."

Her meaningless, add-on phrases turned out to be very meaningful after all. Unfortunately, they communicated that she was "showing the throat" — that is, throwing herself on the mercy of others by saying, "I'm too fragile to get specific about what I mean. Rather than giving to you from inside myself, I'd rather serve you by letting you be in control." Of course, this is not the kind of healthy servanthood called for by our Lord. This is taking the easy way out rather than risking deep engagement with another person.

Padding our sentences with such verbal *escape hatches* signals a willingness to put the other person in charge. The stronger person will fill the vacuum and direct the conversation or the relationship. The advantage to him is that he is free to dominate the other person and to get his expectations met. But the disadvantage is that he is seduced, cajoled into taking care of the weaker person. Further, the weaker one is allowed to stay in a helpless role and becomes chronically dependent in relationships.

Another verbal signal is *self-disparagement*. Recently, I was with a group of Christian men gathered to share stories of how God has worked in our lives. When one man's turn came to talk, he joked around a bit in his preliminary nervousness. He turned to his father (who was present) and said, "I guess I'll tell everyone what a perfect childhood I had and all about my great parents." The group chuckled at this, and the father replied, "Well, when you come to the 'great parents' part, at least you can talk about your mother." Reflecting back on this later, I thought, "Nothing about that little joke invited his son into a deeper relationship with him. Instead of having a relationship, the father would rather meet the group's expectation that he provide tension-relief." The function of his self-disparaging humor was to break the tension introduced by the son's willingness to talk about his childhood with his dad present. This father was "taking care" of the group in an unhealthy way. Meeting others' expectations got in the way of inviting his son into a deeper relationship.

Yet another verbal signal that a person is too open to meet others' expectations is that of over-editing what he says. Have you ever just stopped to "taste" how ponderous and careful someone is as he talks? Do you sense that he is always going through a "mental Rolodex" to find the right word or phrase? Do you hear her interrupt herself with, "No that's not it. That's not what I meant. It's more like this. . . ." The emphasis in this person's conversation with you is not to relate deeply to you, it is to present a perfect package of expression. He or she labors, not to love you well, but to hone the verbal product down to perfection.

Please note this: in this scenario, the other person is not conveying love for you. Rather, he needs you there to endorse the verbal product that is produced. You validate that person's need by engaging in conversation with him and taking him seriously. Yet, responding to this person's desire to be taken seriously *within his compulsion to labor for verbal perfection* is not what he really needs. Ironically, to take him seriously on his own terms *is to fail to love him.*

John was a counselee whose first sentences stunned me with their sophistication. Perfectly edited, they did not match his unkempt appearance. I couldn't have been more unprepared for the polished verbal offerings that flowed from him.

"I think you know my situation," he said as he sat down. I nodded. "Would you be willing," he asked, "to work with me under the auspices of my lawyer? That is, you would be his agent, and if you were to be subpoenaed by the district attorney, you could claim the attorney-client privilege."

Not ready for this barrage of sophistication, I said that I would have to check with a lawyer about the advantages and disadvantages of such an arrangement. Actually, the attorney-client privilege was not the main issue for me at the moment. I began asking myself, "Why this discord between his appearance and his speech?" This was like Elvis singing Handel's "Messiah." The split between John's immediate impact and his polished words worked for him in some powerful ways.

For one thing, I think he enjoyed my internal double take when he began talking. He had set me up, through his appearance, to think he was a bumpkin; and then had surprised me by the polish of his prodigious word power. This was my first hint of his watchfulness. Behind the curtains of his awkward self-presentation, he watched with a smirk as his verbal prowess startled me. An element of revenge haunted our relationship: his awkwardness drew out my subtle contempt, then his smooth words surprised me. He exposed me as a self-satisfied man and thus had his revenge. It was a nice game and well-played. Sensing my internal double take, he enjoyed my brief mental disorientation and, at the same time, validated his own feeling of superiority over me.

Over-editing our conversations almost always constitutes a desire for validation. The sad thing is that if I offer validation to John (or others like him) on his terms, I perpetuate a pattern that badly needs to be exposed and steered in directions that reflect risky loving rather than protective one-upmanship. To fail to interrupt this pattern is to let John continue in a terrible form of bondage. He will not experience real love and will remain a man who is not free and is not loving.

The lack of freedom in this verbal labor communicates an enslavement to perfection. Along with that slavery comes a willingness to work ridiculously hard to meet expectations, both internal and external. This person's fear is, "If I do shoddy verbal work, you might not respect me. If you'll be patient, though, I'll show you how high a standard I can meet."

Further, this verbal labor reflects a fear of being caught in a mistake. This person wants desperately to get everything right lest he be caught in an inaccuracy. His glacier-like conversation shows his over-analysis of everything he says. He is working so hard to meet an impossible standard that he is not really conversing with you; rather, he is in the midst of a pressure-packed dialogue with his own fear of condemnation.

Positional Signals

Still another way to signal that one is too open to expectations from others is through the position one takes in relationships. For example, there is the "one-down" or deferential position. An example of this occurred in a counseling session when I said to my counselee, "You have sought to overcome evil with evil." I had not especially prepared her for this statement. She could not have known with any certainty what I was leading up to. Yet, she responded, "You're talking over my head right now." As she said this, she slumped in her chair and retreated emotionally. She was internally predicting that she was about to feel stupid, and she was waving the white flag ahead of time by saying, in effect, "This is over my head; I'm too dumb to get what you're saying."

I was annoyed. She was taking a *deferential* position that coerced me to assume a superiority that both violated her and confirmed her view of herself as incompetent. If I accepted her destructive view of herself, I would automatically set up a relationship in which she wouldn't have to offer me anything intellectually, so she could adopt the role of meeting my expectations elsewhere in order to have anything to contribute to the relationship. Having disqualified herself as a peer, she had opted to become servile. I could easily fall into her scenario by explaining in condescending detail what I had meant by what I said.

Another type of positional signal of a willingness to meet expectations is that of *permission-seeking*. Here, one person subtly asks to be allowed to say, do, or be something. For example, let's say a husband wants to watch Monday Night Football, but he knows that his wife has signaled him lately that she has not had enough time with him (these signals could be anything from an overt statement of missing him to a covert behavior pattern of yelling at the kids to express indirectly her frustration at him).

He really doesn't want to give her a whole evening, especially not while Monday Night Football is on, so he offers her a token: he cleans up the kitchen after supper. When she walks in after getting the kids in the tub, he says proudly, "How do you like your clean kitchen?" Of course, she is happy to have the kitchen cleaned, but what she really wants is *him*. Nonetheless, he has tacitly asked for permission to let the clean kitchen substitute for his presence so that he can watch Monday Night Football.

His permission-seeking is designed to cover the fact that he prefers to be too weak to meet her real needs: "I don't have what it takes and don't *want* to have what it takes to offer you my real presence in a way that deeply touches you. I would rather present myself as too weak for that. I'll make up for your disappointment by being over-responsive to your expectations in areas that don't require me to be strong and involved."

He develops false guilt feelings that bother him when his wife shows signs of being frazzled. His overactive conscience convinces him that he has not done enough for her, so he goes into overdrive around the house and yard. He does chores, errands, landscaping, repairs, child care— all in an effort to get her to signal him that she is now okay. All along, she senses (if she is honest) that she wants not what he *does* but who he *is*, including a willingness to cultivate his strengths and face his weaknesses in a way that increases his involvement in her life.

THE OVERACTIVE CONSCIENCE GAINS CONTROL BY SACRIFICING EQUALITY

Our Monday Night Football enthusiast is a good example of the fact that an overactive conscience allows the person to be in control. There is a tradeoff: the person with an overactive conscience suffers unnecessary guilt, but in return he gains control. He controls the level of intimacy he offers and receives. He controls the relationships he enters. He controls the level of risk he is willing to endure. In other words, the overactive conscience enables him to design his own comfort zone.

Others read these signals as requests that they express their expectations (some respond to these signals more than others). Most of us instinctively recognize someone who is hungry to earn "merit badges." Thus, those with a conscience filled with false guilt tend to attract those with a high sense of entitlement. The entitled look for the servile, and unfortunately, they often get together. The person with the overactive conscience ends up relating from a "one-down" position. He seeks to be the giver, the appeaser, the one held responsible for how the relationship is going. It looks like a win-lose situation, with the person with the overactive conscience losing. Yet, subtly, the one with the overactive conscience "wins." He wins approval, affirmation, control, predictability, and a relationship with minimal risk. Of course, in the long run, it is a lose-lose situation, because the relationship has no intimacy. In fact, it is not a relationship at all; it is an arrangement.

What the Overactive Conscience Is Trying to Do

THE OVERACTIVE CONSCIENCE has a mission. The *means* for accomplishing that mission is, as we've seen, to maintain a wide-openness to meeting the expectations of others. The conscience filled with false guilt is hungry for expectations. While the methods for accomplishing the mission of an overactive conscience remain fairly consistent, the *purposes* of that conscience are many.

JOB DESCRIPTION OF AN OVERACTIVE CONSCIENCE

The overactive conscience simply has a lot to accomplish. This is why we sense a certain relentlessness in it. The person cannot be allowed to rest because the conscience has a lot to do. It is like a supervisor who is aware of the sheer volume of work his workers have to do. The workers may not see the big picture, but the supervisor does.

Let's see if we can get a handle on the big picture of what a conscience filled with false guilt is trying to accomplish.

Keeps Acceptance Out of Reach

First, the overactive conscience is seeking to keep the "carrot" of acceptance just out of reach. This "carrot" includes self-acceptance and acceptance from others and from God. The guilt-ridden conscience continually says, "Your efforts are not good enough. You must keep trying because, even if your attempts don't measure up, the trying itself counts as something." In this way, we are put on a treadmill: There is plenty of action (trying harder), but we never quite get to our destination (acceptance).

Imagine a stressed corporate executive driving home in his Japanese-made car on a packed, eight-lane commuter beltway. He hardly notices his imprisoning surroundings because of his imprisoning, self-critical thoughts. He is thinking anxiously about a corporate board meeting that ended an hour earlier. He had meant to play a major part in the discussion that followed a crucial presentation at the meeting. If he had been able to score in that discussion, he could have reaped a giant budget increase for his department.

But he had run out of cigarettes! Unbelievably, he had smoked his last cigarette during the actual presentation. When the time came to jump into the discussion, he reached for his pack only to find it empty. How could he stay calm without cigarettes? Shakily, he had tried to run the discussion, but without lighting up and puffing, tapping out the ashes, blowing the smoke out the side of his mouth, without these mechanics he hadn't known what to do with his hands. And they—his hands—betrayed him. They tapped on the table, they scratched in his hair, they wiped his face, they wandered all over his pens, pads, and calculator; they even picked his nose a time or two!

He had felt himself looking like a fool. His hands were his enemies; they were all he could think about. Finally, he jammed them in his pockets and shut up. How can someone dominate if his hands are betraying him? A person has to look confident to carry a discussion, and he can't look confident when his hands are flitting around like nervous finches.

This man is painfully conscious of trying to measure up. He wants to loom large in a discussion. He wants to "score" for his department. He wants to look cool and efficient with his sophisticated cigarette-handling. He wants, in other words, to be accepted. Dominating the discussion, winning the money, looking smooth—these are simply the tools for getting acceptance and validation.

But acceptance and validation are so uncertain. Almost anything can mess it up for him. He runs out of cigarettes, and he's nearly helpless. He feels the acceptance he wants draining through his restless, uncontrollable fingers. He berates himself, "You idiot! I should have made sure I had cigarettes. Next time, I'll have a whole stinking carton. I have to get a new system for keeping track of things, a to-do list, a Day-Timer. Next time, I'll be ready. I'll have to be brilliant to make up for this disaster."

Notice that he doesn't stop and ask himself, "Why did I need to dominate in the first place? And what about this dependence on the mechanics of smoking—is that healthy? What's behind that? What would happen if I didn't have that crutch all the time?" The overactive conscience, in its drive for elusive acceptance, keeps him too busy to look inside. What actually slips through his fingers is a golden opportunity for growth and freedom.

Provides the *Illusion* of Acceptance

The overactive conscience, as we've seen, is seeking to maintain control over intimacy, not letting it get so deep that someone could really know us. On the other hand, total isolation is just as caustic to the soul as the terror of intimacy. Thus, the guilt-filled conscience seeks to provide the *illusion* of acceptance without the risk of intimacy. We are seduced into offering our *hands* to others instead of our *hearts*. What we can *do* for others or God becomes more important than *being* someone who makes others uncomfortably but deliciously thirsty for more. Giving them quantity (the products of our hands) rather than quality (the power and presence of alive hearts) is safer. *And* we believe the illusion of acceptance. Almost *anyone* can be seduced into accepting us (at least superficially) if we *do* enough for them.

Fran, a fifty-ish mother of three grown children, came to the end of her rope in a listless, featureless marriage. My first impression of her was that she had a drive shaft for a spinal column. Efficient, brisk, and smiling in a tight, cool way, she could accomplish more in a morning than I got done in most weeks. I told her that if I wanted to manipulate someone, I would pick her. I knew that I could hitch my wagon up to her, so to speak, and she would dutifully pull me along while I leaned back for the ride.

I went on to tell her that this was exactly what her husband had done. A passive, dependent man, he had recognized quite early in their courtship that Fran would basically fill any vacuum he left in his weak response to life. And he left plenty of them. Sure enough, time and time again Fran dutifully took up the slack—mowing the lawn, calling the plumber, taking care of all the finances, and planning their social engagements and vacations. She could do it, but she was growing weary. And somewhere deep inside a nagging voice was asking, "Is this all there is?"

It took nearly thirty years of marriage for her to wake up to this voice inside. Why? For those thirty years, she had the illusion of acceptance and validity. She thought her duty was to fill whatever gaps her loved ones happened to leave and to clean up all the messes they made. She figured it was worth it to trade all that effort for the affirmation she got in return ("Honey, I don't know what I'd do without you. You amaze me").

But all that acceptance was a mirage. Instead of its

being an oasis for her soul, these words of encouragement were really a signal that her husband didn't want her; he simply wanted the security her caretaking provided. She was not prized and treasured as a human being but as a janitor for his disorderly life. The overactive conscience brings the illusion of acceptance. In reality, the acceptance that is offered is a payment for services rendered. The approving words are simply the wages of unthinking service.

Prevents Any Deep Sense of Rest

The overactive conscience is not happy when I am at rest. Though rest is the birthright of the Christian (Hebrews 3:7–4:13), relaxing is just too dangerous. The guilt-ridden conscience cannot allow me to luxuriate. Relaxing might bring down my guard, then I wouldn't be ready when the face of acceptance turned into the face of shame and rejection (as I fear it will). Rest is dangerous! Others must be monitored for signs of rejection. This leads to a corollary: All acceptance is conditional. It depends on my continuing to prove that I am an asset to others, including God. I can never be a liability if I am to expect acceptance to continue.

False guilt generates a deep weariness. During the Civil War, Abraham Lincoln, when asked how he was holding up under the stresses of leading the nation, said, "Nothing touches the tired spot." This is how the person with an overactive conscience feels. He has a civil war within himself. He is torn between his need for replenishment and his need to demonstrate that he is always an asset. When he relaxes, he feels stressed about relaxing. One woman said, "When I put on the brakes and relax in my life, I get rear-ended by everything that's been chasing me." When I asked what had been chasing her, she replied, "All the things I always need to get done." Her face was a mask of weariness as she spoke.

Offers Me Control

Under the domination of an overactive conscience, my own efforts at handling life become what I trust in; those efforts, rather than God, become my object of faith. A guilt-ridden conscience, then, is a system for handling life that competes with my trusting in the character of God. An overactive conscience offers me a well from which to drink that does not call me out of my comfort zone.

Thus, I stay in control. I live within a framework of self-sufficiency rather than abiding deeply in a relationship with God. Since intimacy terrifies me, especially intimacy with God, I offer Him the same dutiful compliance I give everyone else. I may read and study the Bible, pray, and attend worship services, yet I never allow God to get any closer than I allow anyone else. If He gets too close, I will not be in control any longer. And when control conflicts with intimacy, the latter loses every time.

Keeps a Lid on Evil

My overactive conscience also takes on the job of keeping evil under control. How? By imprisoning evil inside of me! If I am the center of blame and fault in my world, then evil resides uniquely inside me. There it is more contained and controlled (so the illusion goes). Evil is more fearsome as an external marauder we can't control. So, we "control" it by seeing ourselves as the container for evil. When it is inside us, we can seek to control it by compensating for our "unique" badness. We do this by aiming for perfection.

One of my colleagues once related the story of a ten-year-old boy whose mother punished him by making him stand barefoot on a brick patio on a scorching day. The bricks were extremely hot, and he could stand the pain only by hopping from one foot to the other. He kept hopping for over an hour until his mother finally relented.

Who was evil in this story? The mother, of course. Nowhere does the Bible sanction the use of abuse in matters of discipline. Clearly, the mother revealed herself as evil by frying her son's feet for over an hour. But did the son conclude that his mother was evil? Far from it. During his hour of torment, he reasoned, "She's right. I really did blow it. I forgot to bring home my math book for the third time this month. I've just got to do better. I can't keep making Mom mad like this. Look how worried and angry she is. I'm such a jerk, I probably deserve this."

Notice how the overactive conscience extracts evil from outside the child and imprisons it inside him. Suddenly, he is the source of the evil in this situation. Why? Because if evil is "out there," residing in his mother, he can't control it. If she truly harbors evil, then it could strike at any time. But if *he* is the evil one, then he can compensate for it and keep it under wraps by being perfect. He doesn't have to worry about his mother being evil; all he has to do is be extra good, and she will never blow up again.

That night, at the supper table, he apologizes to his mother and to his unaware father, just home from work. He's careful about his manners and goes directly from the table to do his homework. Why? Because he feels that evil is quarantined inside him, cordoned off by all this compliant behavior. He sees his mother's rather stiff smile and says to himself, "See, she's not bad after all. I'm the one I've got to watch." A major legacy of an overactive conscience is that the individual is convinced he is uniquely, shockingly bad.

Provides a Hollow Spirituality
The overactive conscience is afraid of true spirituality. A real walk with God would take me so far out of my comfort zone it terrifies me. I want spirituality that is measurable but not demanding. I want it measurable so I can "prove" to others that I fit into my Christian surroundings. But I refuse the demands of true discipleship, because I sense

that I would have to relinquish control of my life to God.

I want people to *think* that I am bearing fruit, but I do not want the fruit to follow the normal course of nature wherein fruit is borne because of what goes on *inside* the tree. I would rather find a way to hang the fruit on the *outside* of the tree without having to submit myself to God's desire to disrupt and change what is inside me. I prefer a mechanical spirituality that results in merely ornamental righteousness. Mechanical spirituality puts the cart before the horse, insisting on visible righteousness without making sure it comes from internal, invisible dependence on God, who disrupts and changes.

Since our overactive conscience is hungry to meet the expectations of others, we can easily use Christianity to serve our purposes. Since obedience is a pillar of the Christian faith, the guilt-filled conscience allows us subtly to pervert the passion to obey, twisting it into a dutiful, mechanical compliance and conformity. The Bible never envisions a passionless conformity and would not call it obedience. Yet, the overactive conscience is only too happy to utilize the tradition of Christian obedience to justify the presenting of dead compliance as a virtue. Since numb conformity superficially resembles a passionate and grateful obedience, many believers who are driven by false guilt actually pass for mature Christians, at least from a distance.

When you consider all that the overactive conscience motivates us to do, it's no wonder the primary feeling that goes with it is weariness. Laboring to keep acceptance out of reach yet to provide the illusion of it, to prevent any real rest, to keep tight control on life, to clamp a lid on evil by bringing it inside, and to concoct a hollow spirituality that somehow looks convincing—all these things require great energy. The person with false guilt spends much of life simply worn out.

CHAPTER THREE

The Costly Results
of an Overactive Conscience

ALREADY, IT IS EASY to see that the overactive conscience is seeking to establish an entire life-direction and worldview. As I said earlier, it is trying to accomplish a great deal. And it is often able to pull it off. Too often! The ensuing results of its success are desperately tragic.

A CATALOG OF DESTRUCTIVE RESULTS

The overactive conscience keeps me in a state of constant uncertainty. I can never know whether I've arrived or not. I don't, for example, know if I've been *enough* of an asset or done *enough* service or been considerate *enough* of others. In my uncertainty, I must be alert, always on guard for the possible loss of affirmation from others. I am like a commanding general, sending troops here and there in an incessant scurrying to prevent disaster. This effort taxes me deeply. Here are some of the "taxes" I wearily pay as costs of false guilt.

Striving Without Arriving
There is no hope in the system set up by the overactive conscience. I must always *try harder* without ever crossing

the finish line. My internal striving never takes me forward. I go only in a spiral and end up at the same basic place, asking, "Why can't I meet enough expectations to gain a sense of acceptance and significance?" I am always striving without arriving.

Maria told me of being exhausted by the Christmas rush. Unable to extricate herself from it, she had been carried along on a binge of parties, baking, making lists, shopping, children's activities, wrapping, church commitments, and so forth. Her youngest daughter attended a private school that had set up a fund-raising gift-wrap booth at a local mall. She felt she should support this. It would keep tuition costs down, for one thing. So she signed up to wrap gifts four times in December.

In mid-December, the director of the school called in a panic. "We don't have enough people for this Thursday. Everyone is reneging on the times they signed up for. So far, we're a thousand dollars behind what we raised last year. Could you please come on Thursday? I'm counting on you."

Maria had heard the director talk of those who "weren't committed to supporting the school." She didn't want to be one of *those* people. On the other hand, she was exhausted. She felt as though one more commitment would torpedo her already shaky sanity. Yet, what was she to say? She didn't want tuition to go up. She didn't want to be one of the uncommitted. So, she said a halfhearted "yes" and hung up. She tried to quell her anxiety as she thought about rearranging her whole week to accommodate four unforeseen hours of wrapping presents.

Maria is tired of striving without arriving. Notice that she doesn't gain anything by signing up for an extra volunteer session. She simply avoids losing. She avoids losing the good opinion of the director; she avoids breaking her own rule, the one that says she must always be helpful. There is no forward progress, only the arrest of a possible decline. Striving without arriving.

Constant Vigilance

The overactive conscience produces a constant self-monitoring that asks the question, "Am I being an asset to God and others in this situation (as I *must* be)?" Within this system I do not give myself permission ever to be a liability.

One evening I was screening my calls and a voice came on the answering machine saying, "Steve, we're waiting for you to come to speak at our small group. We thought you'd be here by now. We're all here, so I'm calling to check on your status. Hope to see you in the next few minutes." He hung up without leaving a phone number or location. I called a couple of homes where I thought they might be meeting, without success.

The small-group leader had not notified me that the group wanted me to expand on a talk I had given the week before. Although the possibility of my speaking more than once had been mentioned several weeks before, no one had stated, after my initial talk, that there was any need to come back.

Obviously, I had not shown up when expected. This certainly did not make me an asset to the group that night. And, while I need to reflect on whether I had some part in the misunderstanding, it is also important for me to say internally, "It's okay that I'm not being an asset to the group right now. These mistakes happen, and sometimes assets just don't get delivered. This is not a time to feel ashamed." Although I struggled a few times during the evening not to have a shame-filled response and go careening around town, trying to find their meeting, basically I was able to make the above statement. It felt good not to respond with redoubled vigilance, which would have said, "I really screwed up this time. I have to earn my way back into the group's good graces. I'll commit to a whole quarter's worth of Bible studies with them."

Taking a "Pack Mule" Approach to Life

An overactive conscience involves entering a lifelong ordeal. The essence of an ordeal is to pass a demanding test and thus reveal one's true worth. For the guilt-ridden conscience, the test consists of accumulating enough evidences of goodness to escape the accusation that one is worthless. Thus, the person takes on whatever duties, expectations, and roles others seem to want from him. The burdens pile higher and higher. The person is, in effect, a beast of burden, a "pack mule" who accepts far greater responsibility than is healthy or necessary.

Just as there is no forward progress (striving without arriving), there is also an ever-increasing sense of burden. The conscience filled with false guilt demands a fresh supply of validation each day. This person can never rest in saying, "That's enough." She knows she is never enough. So she has to do more.

I told one counselee that he was like a locomotive with thousands of cars attached. Each car was a project, a task, a goal, an assignment, a committee—some form of commitment he had taken on. The tracks on which his train ran were composed of his family. He was using them as rails. Ignored as people, they were good only for supporting him in his endless round of duties. If he was going to be the "pack mule," someone had to be expendable. He couldn't get validation from people who really counted (his boss, coworkers, friends) *and* be there for his family. The "pack mule" approach to life not only exhausts the individual, it also erodes his ties to those closest to him.

A Deep Fear of External Evil

The person burdened with false guilt may feel overwhelmed when he reads or hears accounts of crime, especially those involving violence and cruelty. This person may also be deeply afraid of Satan or demonic activity. Even discussing spiritual warfare can feel overwhelming. Evil that is "out there" feels overwhelming because it is so irrational and unpredictable. It reminds him of the unexpected and excruciating shame experiences of the past, which we'll discuss later. These were times when he felt completely helpless, sprayed with the acid of contempt without warning. External evil—since it carries this same unpredictable, remorseless element—provokes deep fear in the person struggling with false guilt.

He usually handles this fear by getting busy. Prodded by his unsatisfied conscience, he seeks more and better ways of being an asset to those around him. The busier and more seamless his life, the more he can convince himself that badness resides within him and he is conquering it there. What he doesn't want to see is that evil is both "out there" (in others and in the supernatural world) and in himself in different and worse ways than he thought. In parts 2 and 3, I'll develop what I mean by "different and worse."

An Impotent Church

Many Christians struggle with an overactive conscience. The results in the Body of Christ are sobering. The presence of significant numbers of weak, hollow, sweet, and compliant believers results in a church that may be long on unthinking conformity ("I have quiet times because Christian leaders I respect tell me that's what Christians do") and short on passion and substance ("I'm coming to God and His Word because I'm desperate, trembling, and close to falling apart, and I *must* have rest for my troubled soul").

When routine compliance takes the place of passionate obedience, the whole reason for "doing church" shifts radically. The purpose for assembling together becomes that of *displaying the quality of my compliance*. Why? So that I can determine the degree to which I fit in with my Christian surroundings. If I don't "fit," then I won't

be accepted. And gaining acceptance—along with validation—is the central goal of an overactive conscience.

Thus, assembling together as believers often becomes
a massive exercise in gauging whether we fit in enough to
gain the acceptance and validation we crave. This makes
church a place where our central question is, "Do I look
and act enough like those around me to fit in and be
accepted?" instead of asking, "Regardless of how I look and
act, am I passionately worshiping God, deeply thirsting for
Him, and allowing Him to change my relationships so that
I love others in a way that reflects the disruptive sacrifice
of Christ?"

The former question makes church a time of anxiety:
"Am I going to fit in, or am I going to be exposed as an
impostor?" The pressure is on to display the marks of
a successful, maturing believer. When asked how we're
doing, we say, "Fine. The Lord's been gracious." Or, "This
week's been tough, but the Lord is teaching me great
things."

What we rarely say is, "I'm hurting, and I don't know
where to go with it. God seems a thousand miles away,
and I can't find Him." Or, "It's been a tough week. My husband is struggling with his boss, and since he takes it out
on me, my life is really painful."

Recently a woman accosted me after church and asked
in a low whisper, "Is your wife doing better?" I mumbled
something vague about her improvement, and the woman
moved off, seemingly satisfied. I kicked myself inwardly.
I knew I had succumbed to the pressure of making sure
my wife, Susan, and I fit in. Later, I asked my wife why
the woman would have been asking that question. Susan
related that, several weeks before, she had been quite honest with this woman about some deep, personal struggles.
Apparently, the depth of Susan's struggle had bothered
her enough to prompt her approaching me for reassurance that Susan was okay.

It appeared to me that she was checking to see whether Susan was going to fit in or not. My wife's deep struggle had signaled our fellow church member that perhaps something unfit was going on in Susan's life. By checking with me, she was making sure the "unfitness" wasn't continuing. I hasten to add that I believe the woman had some genuine concern as well. But the conspiratorial and anxious tone indicated that my wife's openness had caused insecurity in this woman. And why was she coming to me rather than to Susan? The main point of her conversation with me was to soothe her insecurity, not a desire to figure out how to encourage Susan.

The church is weakened to the degree that it becomes an arena for demonstrating compliance. We become so busy showing our credentials for fitting in and receiving the display of others' credentials that church becomes a place for saying, "I'm okay; you're okay," rather than a place for people who are not okay to come drink from the fountain of Living Water. A relationship with God is medicinal. He assumes that we are sick and wounded. Going to church to say "I'm okay" is, in effect, a way of avoiding Him.

Not only is the guilt-filled conscience a tyrant, its tyranny serves no constructive purpose. It exacts a great toll to produce results that are worse than the tyranny itself. It is like a medieval despot who cruelly taxes his subjects and then uses the revenue to buy pitch and turpentine to burn down their homes. Why do we put up with it? Why do we not dethrone such a tyrant? The answer is that, as cruel as the overactive conscience is, it protects us from something far worse: the acid of shame. The next section explores the source of this conscience and its roots in shame, while part 3 describes the factors that induce us to hang on so tightly to the guilt-filled conscience in spite of its tyranny.

PART TWO

▼

WHERE DID WE GET THIS OVERACTIVE CONSCIENCE?

CHAPTER FOUR

False Guilt Is the *Source* of an Overactive Conscience

MEETING EXPECTATIONS TO GAIN approval and thus fill an empty soul is the mission of the overactive conscience. Picture a busy church secretary surrounded by piles of paper, all of which somehow fit into her job description. She has just gotten off the phone with a shaky woman who discovered her husband is having an affair and who must see one of the church's pastors that day. The secretary must track down one of the pastors to counsel the woman. The secretary herself is juggling projects for all of the pastors, and she faces a Sunday bulletin deadline that is less than three hours away. The phone will ring twelve to fifteen times in those three hours. At this point, a Sunday school teacher rushes in with a teaching outline that must be typed and copied while the teacher waits. On top of that, this teacher has an appointment across town in half an hour.

The secretary has no time to do this. Moreover, the teacher should have typed the outline himself and planned to bring it to the church office at a time when he could drop it off and come back perhaps the next day. The secretary, feeling great pressure, glances at a plaque on the wall. It says, "Poor planning on your part does not necessarily constitute a crisis on mine." She is tempted to refer the demanding teacher to this maxim not five feet away.

But somehow she loses her nerve and finds herself sweetly saying, "Yes, of course." As she types the outline, the bulletin deadline ticks like a bomb in the back of her fevered mind. Why did she give in? It would have been truthful to have said, "I'm sorry, but I simply can't add another thing to my day. My plate is too full as it is. Adding your outline will mean I have to throw the bulletin overboard." Why are these words so dangerous?

It is because she doesn't see the teacher in front of her objectively. Instead, she sees him as either a resource to be tapped or an enemy to be neutralized. As a potential resource, the teacher could be a reservoir of approval and affirmation ("I just marvel at your efficiency. I don't see how you keep up with all of this. You just whipped out my outline without skipping a beat!"). These sentences feel like manna for a hungry soul.

On the other hand, as a potential enemy, the teacher might rob her of what little sense of well-being she has managed to store deep within. The secretary fears that if she refuses to type the outline right then, she might hear caustic disgust: "This church talks about supporting its Sunday school teachers, but I sure don't see it happening," or "I guess Sunday school needs are on the bottom of your list. Where am I supposed to go for help?" Implication: "You have failed me. I will retaliate by withholding patience and kindness."

THE OVERACTIVE CONSCIENCE FINDS SUPPLIES FOR THE EMPTY SOUL

Because of the deep emptiness of her own soul, our secretary is trapped into keeping her supply lines open, either by manipulating the teacher as a resource or placating him as an enemy. Without these supply lines for approval and affirmation, she feels that her soul will starve. The supply lines are, emotionally, a matter of life and death. Our secretary's conscience, then, tells her that it would be selfish of her to refuse to type the outline. By pushing her into compliance, her guilty conscience keeps an "enemy" from materializing. Thus, emotional supplies keep filling her voracious soul.

During the Civil War, Confederate forces drove a Federal army into Chattanooga, Tennessee, after a rebel victory at nearby Chickamauga Creek. Unwilling to press their advantage, the Confederates surrounded Chattanooga on three sides, cut off any adequate supply lines, and waited for the Federal troops to starve or surrender. At this point, President Lincoln called Ulysses S. Grant from his victory at Vicksburg to take command of all Federal troops in the Western theater. Grant rode into Chattanooga, assessed the condition of his scarecrow troops, and decided to blast his way through the Confederates at a point that would allow him to open a supply line and break the rebel stranglehold on his forces. His success in doing so led to eventual victory at Chattanooga and hurried the downfall of the Confederates in the Western theater of operations.

Grant's tactics illustrate how the emptiness of our souls drives us to construe relationships as arenas for self-protective strategy rather than as opportunities to give Christ's love without demanding repayment. Grant knew he had to deal with an enemy to create supply lines. Our secretary dealt with a potential enemy in the same way. She felt she had to meet his expectations to neutralize his potential disgust. Her decision to type the outline had little to do with true servanthood and everything to do with neutralizing an enemy to keep emotional supplies unharmed.

The overactive conscience, then, develops because of a painful void in the soul that aches for filling. Why is the soul so empty? Why is it devastated?

THE EMPTINESS CAUSED BY FALSE GUILT

The projectile that rips through the fabric of the empty soul is false guilt. Note that it has to be false guilt to do damage to the soul. True guilt, which we'll discuss later, does not harm the soul, but false guilt inherently does damage because of where it comes from. The gun that fires the projectile of false guilt is shame—specifically, a kind of shame that covers a person with a suffocating blanket of accusation. The human soul is not meant to be blanketed with indiscriminate shame. Indiscriminate shaming ignores all that is attractive about a soul and implies that a soul can be wrong, not only for what it does but for the fact that it exists.

INDISCRIMINATE SHAME AT WORK

Let me show you how indiscriminate shame harms the deepest, most vulnerable parts of a human being. When my oldest daughter, Katy, was six, she had developed a manipulative way of responding to bedtime. (Has any other parent ever had this problem?) She would think of a dozen "needs" that somehow hadn't occurred to her until the lights were out. They ranged from "needing" a drink of water to "needing" an extra hug.

One night, when I had come home particularly weary, she pulled an unusually drawn-out series of "Dad, I need this . . . Dad, I need that" at bedtime. I felt too whipped to deal firmly with the manipulation at its first appearance. Instead, I grudgingly complied with her requests, hoping each time that she would relent and go to sleep. My resentment swelled a bit more at each summons.

Finally, when she accosted me in the kitchen with, "Dad, can you adjust the fan?" I exploded, "Get back in that bedroom! I can't believe you! This is ridiculous! Give me a stinking break!" My tone was vicious, my face twisted in rage. Her eyes widened. Her face fell. Her frame slumped. She turned to walk back to her room. I followed, ready to nail her if she so much as breathed sideways.

I was ready for more of the same manipulation (I'd have wiped it out), but I was not ready for what followed. Before reaching her room, she turned, fixed me with sad eyes and said, "Dad, when you talk to me that way, I feel so stupid inside."

Now, put yourself in my role as father. Think through what would be some bad sentences to say to Katy at this point. Look up from this book and say those damaging sentences aloud to feel the magnitude of their impact.

Some damaging sentences might be . . .

"I don't care how you feel. Your job is to get to bed right now!"
"You *should* feel stupid. You're the one who won't go to sleep."
"Don't back-talk me, young lady!"
"I'll give you something to feel stupid about!"
"Your feelings are not the issue. Your behavior is the problem."

Such words jar and tear the soul in frightening ways. Perhaps you can think of times when, as a child, you heard similar words.

Now, think of some constructive words for Katy. Say them aloud.

Some positive sentences might be . . .

"I really hurt you, didn't I?"
"You're right. The way I talked to you was wrong."
"I really wasn't responsible with my words and tone. I know I get demanding when I'm tired."
"What do you think of when I talk to you that way?"
"Do I talk to you that way a lot when I'm tired?"
"Honey, you're right. I need your forgiveness."

These kinds of responses create a place for the soul to relax and communicate instead of warding off the acid of shame.

SHAME AND THE IMAGE-BEARER

Katy is made in the image of God, as all of us are. The Bible sees human beings from two broad perspectives: dignity and depravity. Since we are made in the image of God, we are, even as fallen beings, repositories of glory and honor. For example, David, after noting the smallness of humans in comparison with the creative greatness of God, says of man, "Yet Thou hast made him a little lower than God, and dost crown him with glory and majesty!" (Psalm 8:5). Note that these lines were written *after* humankind's fall into sin, describing something that is true about people even in their fallen state.

Clearly, humans—made in God's image—are still enough like God to be objects of admiration, even though because of our depravity we are not objects of merit. Because we bear the image of God, we are worthwhile; but because we are depraved, we are not worthy. This is why Francis Schaeffer has said, "Man is a glorious ruin."

Humankind: A Glorious Ruin

Man is like a castle that has gradually fallen down around itself. Yet a visitor, chancing upon such a castle in the English countryside, might yet discern the outlines of grandeur in the cracked lines that used to soar but which still hint of glory. A diarist in Charleston, South Carolina, watching Fort Sumter absorb an artillery pounding, penned this: "That ruin is beautiful. But it is more than this, it is emblematic also. . . . Is it not in some respects an image of the human soul, once ruined by the fall, yet with gleams of beauty and energetic striving after strength . . . ?"

Scripture is uncompromising in painting humans with

the twin brushes of dignity and depravity. Every child, from the moment of conception, is an amalgam of dignity (image-bearing) and depravity (fallenness). Every child, then, needs a parenting style that takes *both* realities into account.

The Potency of Shame

All parents keep a potent weapon in their parenting arsenal. It is called shame. The parental instinct to shame a child is powerful. If you can get shame to stick to a certain undesirable behavior or attitude, that behavior will usually disappear. In other words, whatever you can shame, you can cause to retreat.

Under some circumstances, shame can be a wise counter-force to evil and foolishness in children. After all, we don't want our children to be *shameless.* But if shame is applied indiscriminately, if shame is applied without making a clear distinction between dignity and depravity, it can be frightfully toxic to the soul. Most parents do not faithfully distinguish between dignity (which is not meant to bear the acid of shame) and depravity (which can be shamed as long as the truth is spoken in the context of a loving relationship).

This represents a parenting style that makes the distinction:

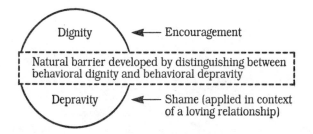

Instead of this constructive approach to using shame, parents—failing to detect the dignity embedded in much of their children's behavior—all too often employ a style

of parenting that uses shame as an all-purpose discipli-
nary tool.

The other day, I heard a mother in the grocery store
say to her young daughter, "If you don't stop looking
at those flowers, I'm going to call grandmother and tell
her you didn't want to come, because you'd rather see
the flowers than her." She might as well have given the
child a bath in acid. All of a sudden, a perfectly inno-
cent activity (looking at the beauty of flowers) becomes
evidence that she doesn't love her grandmother! How different if the mother had said, "Honey, those flowers are
beautiful, aren't they? You're right to admire them. But
we're in a hurry to get to grandmother's. How about if we
look at them next time we're here?" Instead, the parent's
shaming response treated the child as one big hunk of
depravity. Even looking at flowers becomes wrong and
somehow an attack on grandmother. What a wicked child!
The mother completely failed to distinguish between dignity and depravity and dumps the acid of shame on both,
as this diagram depicts:

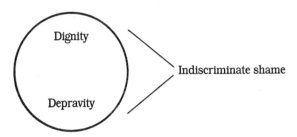

BEING WISE WITH THE HUMAN SOUL

Most parents never develop that shame-proof barrier pictured in the diagram on page 45, partly because they have
never felt that barrier applied to *them*. Few relationships
are places where others are wise and careful with the

intricacies of the human makeup. Many of us have never felt another person relating to us out of a thoughtful understanding of that for which we are designed. We are *not* designed to be shamed for our dignity, for bearing the image of God.

When Katy turned to me and said, "Dad, when you talk to me that way, I feel so stupid inside," she had shifted—in the blink of an eye—from expressing depravity to offering me her dignity. She knew instinctively that she was not built for viciousness from her father, not even when she was at fault for manipulating him. Firmness from me—especially when she first began manipulating me—would not have harmed her. But my reaction of viciousness bypassed her behavior and attacked her being. Deep inside, she knew that she was being wronged, so she shifted into expressing her dignity in a legitimate way.

To be the parent God designed me to be, *I had to make the shift with her.* When a child shifts to an expression of dignity and a parent doesn't, the result will be a shaming attack on the child's dignity. Because of this application of false shame and guilt, the child may develop an overactive conscience, seeking to fill the painful void in the soul.

WHEN SHAME IS FELT AS CORROSIVE

Shame that fails to distinguish between dignity and depravity is felt by the child as contempt. Contempt is corrosive to the soul, an acid that says, "You are a flaw as a human being. Your presence is laughable." When people are treated as not worth the effort it takes to distinguish between their foolish wrongdoing and the design in their souls, they are tempted to believe that their essential existence is bad. They feel bad for existing, although the Bible never says that it is bad that we exist. Scripture teaches that we are "dead in our trespasses and sins," but God *never tells us that it is bad we are here.* Rather, He says, for example, that He takes no pleasure in the death of the wicked. Even when rebellious men and women die apart from Him, He grieves. Why? Because the existence of a human being is of such import to Him that He sorrows to see it wasted.

Indiscriminate shame, on the other hand, says, "Your very presence is offensive. You are an irritant to me. I'd be better off if you weren't here." The damaging responses I could have given to Katy (page 43) would have conveyed that she was a mistake, that it simply was not good for her to be here. This kind of shame says, "No one in his right mind would want you around. There is nothing good about you, *not even your existence.*"

THE DAMAGE OF SHAMING THE ESSENCE OF MALENESS OR FEMALENESS

Negative shaming can take a slightly different but equally destructive form when it is aimed, not so much at a person's existence, but at his or her *existence as a male or a female.* When a child feels that his or her *gender* is a mistake, that child feels deep shame about being born male or female. Many women, for example, feel that their femininity is a terrible flaw. This may have begun if they were told (directly or indirectly) at an early age that one or both parents were disappointed at having a daughter.

Perhaps the girl was given a masculine name as in the case of Jean whose father's name was Gene. He made it clear that giving his daughter the name "Jean" was a masculinizing of her that expressed his disappointment that she couldn't be "a real boy." Striving to be a "real boy," led her to develop an unnatural, guttural voice, to swear often, and to dress exclusively in jeans.

As Jean and I moved into these signals that something was amiss in her femininity, she raised a curtain that revealed deep-seated scorn for something inside her that was actually demure and modest. Musing on the roots of this scorn, she remembered an incident that happened when she was beginning to develop into a woman at puberty. She had been getting ready to go to school one morning when her father entered her room without knocking. Clad only in pants, she folded her arms in front of her developing breasts and turned modestly away with a pained expression on her face. His response was swift and cutting: "Oh, aren't we the prim and proper one?! Too modest for your dad all of a sudden?" The mocking voice conveyed to her that she could have no control over the level of modesty and privacy she needed as she wrestled with the question, "Is it okay that I'm becoming a woman? Is it all right that I'm more and more undeniably a female?"

When her father ridiculed the screen of privacy, he assailed her for needing the cocoon of modesty in which to develop a secure femininity. The child he wanted—a "real boy"—he implied, would be brazenly comfortable in displaying his torso. Jean's moving toward modesty conveyed to her father that she was rejecting his masculine role for her. Rather than acknowledging his pain over that, he poured the acid of shame on what was never meant to endure shame—i.e., her femininity.

When shaming finds a target that was never intended to bear shame, that target recoils from the acid (remember, whatever can be shamed will be caused to retreat). Jean retrieved her shocked and agonized femininity, tucking it away behind an increasingly strong masculine identity. It should be no surprise that within a few years of that incident (and others like it), she was involved in a lesbian relationship.

SHAME FORCES A DECISION

Indiscriminate shame puts the human soul at a fork in the road. This is an especially crucial juncture in childhood. The child must decide whether to insist on the fact that he has a design. To so insist is one of the riskiest moves a person can make. Why? Because of what we are designed *for.*

The Dilemma of Being Made for Paradise

Because we are made in God's image, we are designed for *paradise* and we are designed for *people.* In part, *paradise* describes a world that is in tune with and responds to our initiatives. It is a place where we can make a clear, enjoyable, and helpful impact. This present world, antithetically, is not responsive to our initiatives. In fact, the curses issued in Genesis 3 tell us that our initiatives are going to meet with thorns and thistles, not with fruit.

Thorns and thistles are a picture of complication and frustration. God tells Adam in Genesis 3:17-18, "Cursed is the ground because of you. . . . Both thorns and thistles it shall grow for you." With these words, God abolishes paradise. Instead, the world is shaped so that human effort and initiative become painful, intercepted by God's wise curse. No longer does the garden melt to Adam's touch. No longer can he count on a cooperative environment. Instead of being welcomed by his world, he is now opposed. Now he gets his food "in toil" and "by the sweat of [his] face." Every fruit he eats is wrested from the ground. The earth lets it go only reluctantly and only after exacting a pound of flesh and a quart of sweat.

Fruit is hard to come by in a fallen, sinful world, especially the fruit of mature, godly character. And not just the sod under our feet is cursed, the soil of the human heart is also cursed and hard. It yields fruit sparingly. Only under the operation of God's grace can a heart be softened and yield much fruit. This is why Christ tells us that the seed that falls on the good ground bears "fruit, thirty, sixty, and a hundredfold" (Mark 4:20). Clearly, having our heart softened by Christ mitigates some of the effects of the curse.

The softening of individual human hearts is the divine prelude to God's creation of a whole new Heaven and earth. Paradise is coming again on a massive scale! For now, God uses His grace to recreate the human heart so that His softened people can exude the aroma of paradise throughout the wasteland of fallen humanity that stretches as far as the eye can see.

The Dilemma of Being Made for People

Exuding the aroma of paradise to others indicates that we are not only designed to have a special place (paradise), we are also built for people. We long for paradise, and we long for people with whom we can give and receive unconditional love. We are built for deep, unreserved contact. God designed us for intimacy.

What happens when we live out this design? Again, an illustration will help. Mary was muddling through a colorless marriage, when she sought counseling for depression and marital conflict. In the course of our chats, she revealed that her husband frequently woke her up in the middle of the night for sex. For years, she simply complied, not wanting to rock the boat and vaguely applying 1 Corinthians 7, which encourages mates not to withhold sex from each other (except for appointed times of prayer).

But as she explored her feelings about her husband's sexual habits, she began to get in touch with deep shame and anger. Why? Aside from the inconvenience involved, is there any reason to question her husband's treatment of her? What did her husband's approach to sex convey to her? It conveyed that her value lay in the fact that she had the right plumbing to gratify his sexual needs. At two o'clock in the morning, she was not a deeply loved, cherished, feminine woman for whom her husband had deep respect. She was simply a service-provider. Was this consistent with her deep desire to be loved unconditionally? Obviously not.

Gradually, she began to insist that she and her husband develop a sex life that would convey to her that he thought of her as a precious person and not just as a nice arrangement of plumbing. Her insistence that he recognize *the design of her soul* met with angry resistance. He sought to make her feel guilty for asking for a more respectful sexual relationship. He began to mock her efforts to get help through counseling: "Why are you getting this counseling? You've talked to people about your problems before. Why should it help this time? You're just a junkie for spilling your guts to somebody." She found his contempt excruciating. She was tempted to return to business as usual so that his scorn would stop blistering her soul. Contempt withers human dignity.

The price for living out our design is often astronomical. This is why it is tempting to live according to the lie of indiscriminate shame—a lie that says, "You have no design. You could have nothing that significant about you. You're a zero. It's too bad you're here." Or alternatively, "It's too bad you're here as a man or as a woman."

Although the message that we have no intrinsic design is extremely painful, it is less painful than the scorn that often comes when we live by our design as image-bearers. Scorn that comes from those who purport to love us is devastating. Mary became a target for scorn from her own husband when she sought to live by her design as a woman. By denying her design, she could quiet the scorn. She could go back to doing business as usual. She could appear to have a "good" marriage, which was actually a mockery of God's design for marital intimacy.

The most effective way to deny our design is to shame ourselves for wanting to be loved and cherished. Indiscriminate shame causes our true design to recoil in pain and eventually to go numb. Thus, Mary could use shame to numb her own soul (which should never be shame's use). She could assault her own soul and avoid revealing her fragile, but God-given, hopes for a world where her soul would be cherished.

RESPONDING TO SHAME BY BEGGING FOR ANOTHER CHANCE

Not only does internally shaming oneself forestall the agony of dashed hope, it also provides a way to beg for another chance at being loved. The reasoning goes something like this: "Okay, I agree that I'm a liability. It's *not* good that I'm around; I really *shouldn't* be here, and I apologize for taking up space. Having said that, perhaps I could get permission to hang around in life by making up for my flaws. Just tell me what you want, and I'll live up to it. Maybe that way I can buy some sense of belonging." In this way, we embark on a path of emotional acquisition; the overactive conscience takes over, looking for approval and validation.

On this path of emotional acquisition we are saying, "Maybe you'll let me be here if I can give you all you want. I'll let you use me if I can be a parasite on you." What does the parasite want? Since he believes that his very existence is a bad joke, he wants strong assurance that if he can be good enough, he can gain a feeling of validity, of really belonging to the human race. He wants to go from being a laughingstock to being accepted.

What capital can he spend to acquire the status of being accepted? The only capital he has is his ability to meet the expectations of others. He liberally spends this capital in a desperate effort to acquire the status he wants.

In a word, he becomes *acquisitive*. He incessantly looks for opportunities to spend his capital—i.e., to meet the expectations of others. He literally uses relationships to buy the validity he craves. He becomes an opportunist. He sees people not as human beings but as opportunities to barter for goods. Relationships become places of exchange. The sacred ground whereon he is to seek to love others instead becomes a marketplace of buying and selling.

He becomes greedy, even voracious. The compulsive filling of the emptiness inside dominates him, his loved ones, and his friends. He creates a web of supply sources, at the center of which he is a black hole. Walker Percy, the novelist, refers to this way of living as built around the "suck of self." He describes modern man as "a self sucking everything into itself."[1] Percy's words drive home the idea that we are all greedy. We crave the emotional goodies that others "owe" us.

THE OVERACTIVE CONSCIENCE SEEKS ACQUISITION

The acquisitive person has decided which fork in the road to take. Conversely, the road less traveled is that of dignity, the road of hope based on design as an image-bearer. Acknowledging design brings hope because if I have a design, then there must be a Designer who knows how to quench the thirst of my soul. The other road—the one our traveler has now taken—is that of depravity, the road that self-protectively denies design and elevates acquisition. The overactive conscience is the spur that gives energy to fill the empty, hungry place inside. It goads with false guilt, saying, "You must always be an asset, never a liability. You must always have something to give, and never be needy."

Underneath this false guilt is the desperate fear that, if we stop for one moment giving others what they want, we'll be assaulted by the voice of shame, accusing us that we really are a joke as human beings. If we don't give at all times, what else could we possibly have to offer? The voice of shame has a ready answer, "You have nothing to offer because you are a nothing, a flaw, a blot on the earth. If you stop giving for one second, you'll be laughed at. You'll

be scorned and driven away into nothingness." False guilt
is our frantic attempt to keep this voice quiet. If we can
keep striving, driven by a consciousness of guilt even for
living as such a flawed being, maybe the voice of shame
will be hushed.

The following is a firsthand account of the relentlessness of an overactive conscience driven by false guilt. It
is taken from the journal of one of my counselees and is
used by permission:

> Lately, I've noticed several "pockets" of "validation-
> seeking" or "approval-seeking" in my life. . . .
> With . . . , [I'm not] truthful with them when they
> give me last-minute projects with no lead time. . . .
> With . . . , he's driving me nuts hanging around
> the office and it's because I won't confront him
> and say I don't have time to chat right now. . . .
> [Not only this but] every single lunch next week
> is booked with someone. . . . I need lunch for *me*
> to unwind or be quiet or alone. That seems so
> wrong to me not to give-give-give. Christians are
> to lay down their lives for the brethren, aren't
> they? Where's the line drawn? Are we supposed
> to preserve energy? Jesus went away from the
> crowds to pray. . . . I feel like everyone wants a
> piece of me and I want my pieces for myself. Isn't
> that selfish? I feel like it is. . . . Instead of seek-
> ing approval from these people by not saying "no"
> or "that's too much" or "I need more time," etc.,
> I need to see that my approval is in Christ, and
> I don't think I do, or I wouldn't keep doing this,
> would I?

The agony of soul is clear as this lovely woman struggles to shed the bonds of an overactive conscience. She is
moving away from being enslaved to the expectations of

others, but she is insecure as to what awaits her. Will she become selfish? Will others want her anymore? Is there a path toward both freedom and making everyone happy? She knows there's no such path, but she is afraid not to give the pieces of her everyone demands. Her guilt-driven conscience keeps butting in, insisting that she give all the pieces that others want. Is there another way to get the approval she so desperately craves?

A few days later, she makes the following entry, a prayer:

> Lord,
> Help me to relax and be at peace with who I am—a woman who is needy and overwhelmed. . . . I can't fake it. I can't change it. I can only surrender to it. Lord, help me to face my needs and longings, to ask for help and receive it. . . . Help me . . . provide an atmosphere in which the men around me are helped not to be avoiders. Lord, will I ever feel okay? This confusion, etc., is so hard. Part of me wants to take control, but part of me says, "No, stay free from that. You don't have to live like that anymore." Lord, I'm going to cease striving and know You are God. Amen.

Do you hear the plate tectonics in this woman's soul? The shifts are continental in size and filled with wonder and beauty. She is moving from a stiff, rigid, and angry compliance to a freedom that allows her even to entertain the goal of providing "an atmosphere in which the men around me are helped not to be avoiders." How many women have that as a conscious goal? Only the ones who are seeking to be free from an overactive conscience. Instead of being a slave to expectations, this woman wants freedom to be a helpmeet to her husband (see Genesis 2:18). She wants to be free to help the men around her (beginning with her husband) with the issues of their character.

If you read back over her first entry, you can hear false guilt seeking to confuse the issue: "Christians are supposed to lay down their lives for the brethren, aren't they?" While nothing could be more wonderfully true, the question is "What does it mean to lay down your life?" Certainly, laying down your life does not include sucking on others for constant approval. A person can put the mask of Christian service over the greed of the insecure self. Nonetheless, once unmasked it can be seen for what it is: a parasitic commitment to draw others into a web of emotional acquisition.

False guilt is a driver, a tyrant. It threatens us with shame if we don't meet expectations wherever we find them. Further, and even worse, false guilt promotes a cycle that guarantees a deepening enslavement.

CHAPTER FIVE

False Guilt Is the *Aim*
of an Overactive Conscience

FALSE GUILT IS THE driving force behind an overactive conscience. Indiscriminate shame makes me feel wrong for living and puts me on the treadmill of atoning guiltily for the fact that I am alive. Once I rule out the road less traveled (that of hope based on my design as an image-bearer), I embark on the road of appeasing others, because they are—at least potentially—unhappy that I am around. And if they aren't overtly unhappy, I must prevent their becoming so. In order to remain inoffensive, I must stay on the shame–false-guilt cycle:

Shame
("It is bad that you are here")
↓

False Guilt
("It *is* bad that I am here; I *am* bad")
↓

Overactive Conscience
("I must make amends for my badness by being
a nonstop asset for others")

As long as I am on this cycle, I function on a hidden agenda (hidden even from myself): "I must generate the false guilt necessary to fuel my overactive conscience. That way, I'll never have to face the fear of what might happen if I stop being an asset."

Bill is a friend of mine who has lived through this cycle countless times. Recently, he told of a situation in which his wife had been asked to substitute teach a Sunday school class. She agreed to do so and then, being unsure of her teaching abilities, asked Bill to help her with the class.

His first reaction was to feel a wave of obligation crash over him. He felt a compulsion that shouted, "You *have* to do this. Your wife is counting on you. You have no freedom to decline. If you do, she'll be disappointed in you." This is the raw, accusing voice of the overactive conscience. This internal nagging often served to goad Bill into compulsive service for others. He didn't serve out of a genuine desire to help others, he served in order to get his head out of the noose of false guilt that his guilt-driven conscience was tightening around his neck. Serving in this way, however, *doesn't take the noose away.* Bill is still on the gallows; he simply gets a temporary reprieve by agreeing to the other person's request. His acquiescence simply heightens his fear of what he has avoided: the noose of false guilt. The result is that false guilt becomes even more pivotal as the motivating force in Bill's life.

THE CRUEL REPRIEVE
OF AN OVERACTIVE CONSCIENCE

Changing the metaphor a bit, Bill's inner sensation is similar to that of a death-row inmate who has just learned of an eleventh-hour stay of execution. He is, so to speak, sitting in the electric chair, sweaty-palmed and nauseated, when the wall phone rings with the news of the reprieve. His relief is deep but not total. He is off the hook only for a short while. He returns, not to freedom, but to a cell.

The person with an overactive conscience lives in that death-row cell. The desired reprieve comes from responding to the voice of that guilt-driven conscience. For Bill, this response could mean only one thing: He had to help his wife teach the class. Only then could he be sure he had avoided the noose of false guilt. His words were both sad and illuminating: "I felt as though not teaching the class would confirm that I am a liability. The disappointment in my wife's eyes would inflict the shame I felt as a boy. Disappointing others always meant that there would be some sort of trial to decide whether I really belonged in the family."

He went on to tell of the time he made a "C" on his report card (the rest of the grades were "A's" and "B's"), and his father lectured him unmercifully, telling him, at one point, that "it was Communist to bring home such a bad grade." Bill had no clue what a Communist was or what it had to do with bad grades, but his father's tone communicated clearly: "If you don't watch out, you will prove how despicable you are. And if you are going to act out your despicable nature, I'm not sure I want you around."

Bill remembered well the six agonizing weeks until the next report card. In those weeks he had to prove he deserved a stay of execution. His agony turned to elation when he discovered five "A's" and a "B" on his next report card. His father's response? Was it delight? Was it a reflective apology for his insensitivity of six weeks before? Not on your life! His father's words were, "That's more like it." He reluctantly put down the noose, and Bill felt deeply the absence of any delight from his dad. Bill knew that the reprieve was both halfhearted and temporary. He would have to keep working to earn his place in the home. The noose was still handy.

False guilt, then, is a stern warden who intones,

"You've gotten only a reprieve, mind you. You are not free. You must be ready on short notice to prove that you deserve further reprieves as time goes on." This is how the shame–false-guilt–overactive-conscience cycle becomes self-maintaining. There is no redemption *within* the cycle. That is, the cycle contains only the seeds of continuing slavery.

HOW AN OVERACTIVE CONSCIENCE IS CULTIVATED

An overactive conscience, then, is not really something we *get*. Rather, it is something we *develop*. We develop a guilt-driven conscience *from* the raw material of early shame. We maintain it *for* the purpose of generating more false guilt. False guilt, in turn, deepens our inner sense of shame. Self-generated shame is strategically helpful. With it, we can continue to neutralize our design as image-bearers. *We would rather live in the dull pain of self-contempt than in the acute pain of violated design.* Unfortunately, the former is the path to death; the latter, the path to life.

False Guilt Keeps Hope at Bay

An overactive conscience, then, stems from hidden realities in the soul, realities that revolve around early shame, false guilt, and self-generated (though now strategic) shame. Since false guilt is the member of this trio that we most often feel, let's use it again as the centerpiece of looking at the shame cycle from another angle. Not only does false guilt ensure that we never escape the prison of accusation-condemnation-reprieve, it also ensures that we never give in to the lure of hope.

We have a strategic commitment to maintain false guilt, because it neutralizes the dangerous hope that arises when we acknowledge our God-given design. How does false guilt neutralize the hope that we might be more than the scumball we feel we are? Mainly by attacking truth, especially the truth as revealed by God in Scripture. False guilt labors to nullify troublesome truth from outside us, truth that may awaken us to our design and wreck the carefully cultivated weeds in our otherwise desolate garden.

False Guilt as a Competing "Truth-System"

When we feel false guilt, it is because we need it as a "truth-system" to intercept the truth as God reveals it. Romans 6:1-13 gives a framework for understanding how our hidden "truth-system" interferes with the truth of God's words to us:

> What shall we say then? Are we to continue in sin that grace might increase? May it never be! How shall we who died to sin still live in it? Or do you not know that all of us who have been baptized into Christ Jesus have been baptized into His death?
>
> Therefore we have been buried with Him through baptism into death, in order that as Christ was raised from the dead through the glory of the Father, so we too might walk in newness of life. For if we have become united with Him in the likeness of His death, certainly we shall be also in the likeness of His resurrection, knowing this, that our old self was crucified with Him, that our body of sin might be done away with, that we should no longer be slaves to sin; for he who has died is freed from sin. Now if we have died with Christ, we believe that we shall also live with Him, knowing that Christ, having been raised from the dead, is never to die again; death no longer is master over Him. For the death that He died, He died to sin, once for all; but the life that He lives, He lives to God. Even so consider yourselves to be dead to sin, but alive to God in Christ Jesus.

Therefore do not let sin reign in your mortal body that you should obey its lusts, and do not go on presenting the members of your body to sin as instruments of unrighteousness; but present yourselves to God as those alive from the dead, and your members as instruments of righteousness to God.

The passage revolves around three great commands: "know" (verse 6—the fact that the word in the text, "knowing," is a participle does not interfere with its being a command), "consider" (verse 11), and "present" (verse 13).

Christians often feel frustrated in trying to carry out these three commands. The first one is not too difficult; most of us can bring ourselves to the point where we *know* that an old part of us has been assaulted by the death of Christ. The passage says that this part of us is the "old self" (literally, "old man") and that the assault of Christ's cross has crucified it. This has happened, we are told, in order "that our body of sin might be done away with." The idea is that our body is the instrument through which sin expresses itself (this would include all features of our physical nature, including our brains, senses, and limbs) and that, since the old self is crucified, it is possible to do away with ("render powerless") the body as a channel through which sin expresses itself.

Thus, my physical body (and all it includes) can be rendered powerless as a instrument for sin and can now "come alive" as an instrument of righteousness. Not only has there been a death (of the old self), there is also a new aliveness (explained in verses 8-10) because of our new relationship with God through Christ.

Knowing Versus Reckoning

So far, so good. These are things we can know conceptually. But then we run into verse 11: "Even so consider yourselves to be dead to sin, but alive to God in Christ

Jesus." Some other translations use the word *reckon* instead of *consider*. Either way, the idea is that we are to declare something to be true about ourselves and prepare to live on the basis of it. Yet, many Christians have stumbled here. At the point of being mastered yet again by some sinful habit, they have reckoned themselves dead to sin. In desperation, they consider it to be so. They claim it. They pray desperately for the willpower to declare it true. And still they fall prey to the same old sinful habit.

Then they despair: "I did what Romans 6 says to do, and I still failed! What's wrong with me? Could it be that somehow I'm not a believer at all?" I've said these words myself in dark desperation. And my heart breaks at the number of Christians who have accepted defeat and written off Romans 6 and other passages like it. They feel disloyal to God's Word, yet it hasn't "worked" in their lives. They wonder what's missing.

The Competing Declaration that False Guilt Makes

I'm delighted to say that something *is* missing when Romans 6:11 doesn't "work." In other words, when it doesn't seem to help to reckon ourselves dead to sin, there is a reason. *We can reckon something to be true only when we are not reckoning some conflicting idea to be true at the same time.* We cannot successfully declare ourselves to be dead to sin when false guilt prompts sin to be very much alive in us, alive in the form of assaulting our design with indiscriminate shame. Again, we cannot reckon competing truths to be true. We must reject and repent of false "truth-systems," including those of our own making. False guilt is a "truth-system" cultivated from early shame messages and intended to generate new shame in order to kill our longing for a world that would recognize our God-given design. We cannot be involved in the murder of our own design and at the same time reckon ourselves to be dead to sin.

The following chart highlights how vaguely felt, but powerful "truths" generated by false guilt can compete with scriptural truth:

SCRIPTURAL TRUTH	CONFLICTING "TRUTH"
You are identified with the death of Christ and thus free to disengage yourself from the power of sin.	You are identified with the fact that your identity is shameful; you have no right to disengage from sin, because sin brings the kind of shame you are doomed to live under.
You are now free to act with the hope that you are designed for something radically different than shame — i.e., it is possible to love and to want to be loved in a way that brings a new awareness of Christ into the world.	You must kill or numb any part of your soul that wakes up to its longing to be loved without strings attached — i.e., to be loved as Christ would love.

REPENTING OF THE "DEEPER RECKONING"

In order for us to reckon ourselves dead to sin, we must repent of a deeper reckoning that we have known since childhood. This deeper reckoning says, "It is a shame that you are alive. One false move and people are going to reject you with the same corrosive shame you endured years ago. So watch your step." Or, "Your gender is shameful and a dreadful mistake. One false move and you'll reveal the parts of your masculinity or femininity that you're so ashamed of. And then people will humiliate you for those ugly parts of your soul. So watch your step."

How the "Deeper Reckoning" Works in the Real World

This deeper reckoning works itself out in dreadful ways. Catherine has struggled with lesbianism for fifteen years. Her inner world is a raging war between two bitter rivals.

On one side is her built-in hope for a cherishing tenderness, especially from men. This hope springs from her design as a woman. On the other side is a masculinized woman who is hard, matter-of-fact, and angry. This part of her lives to crush the hope for tenderness that wrestles to be free.

Catherine was sexually abused at age nine by a weak father who was too fearful to approach his wife for a healthy sexual relationship. His impotence was looking for a safe place to feel powerful. It was easier for him to grab some counterfeit potency at his daughter's expense than to require his wife to look at her sexual ambivalence. The message that Catherine heard in all this was, "Men will always opt for sex over risky relational involvement." Yet she longed for a tender, cherishing, yet strong relational involvement—exactly what her father refused to provide.

At first, Catherine sought that kind of involvement from other men. Her dating relationships consisted of a quest for intimacy, tenderness, and cherishing. To her deep dismay, almost every man she dated (including Christians) soon sexualized the relationship. Over and over, she would hope that, this time, a man would respond to her as a woman who legitimately hoped to be cherished and respected. Over and over, she would retreat in disgust as various men treated her in essentially the same way her father had.

Since loving, respectful involvement didn't seem to be available from men, Catherine turned to women for love and tenderness. Tragically, she had learned from her father's abuse that sex was something she could offer to entice others to love her. She was willing to offer sexuality if another would show her the tenderness she craved (men typically had not been tender, or they had been tender only as a prelude to sex). When women, in contrast, offered her emotional intimacy, she responded by sexualizing the relationship. This was her way of enticing the other woman to stay. This cycle led to lesbian relationships through her twenties and thirties.

The availability of tenderness and respect from women tempted her to believe a powerful lie: "You are a fool to expect a man to want anything but sex from you. Because of your femininity, all you can offer a man is receptive plumbing. And that's all they want. What a joke to think that there is anything special a man might see in a woman." This first internal declaration competed directly with any attempt to declare herself dead to sin. Its mocking, jeering tone was fused with the false guilt that Catherine felt over being a woman.

This led to yet another lie: "If I hadn't been a woman, my father would never have had sex with me. He would have turned to my mother, and they would have been happy. The fact that I am female ruined my parents' marriage." This was a second declaration. Angry about the danger inherent in her femaleness and about the weakness she experienced in men, she added a third declaration: "The only way to get anything good out of femaleness is to offer sexuality to women who will be tender toward me." In other words, her femininity would be advantageous only to the degree she could pervert it.

In her mid-thirties, on the verge of her third lesbian relationship, Catherine sought desperately to declare herself dead to the sin of homosexuality as Romans 6 commanded. For a while, she was able to "white-knuckle" it, forcing a discipline upon the raging voice inside that said, "Your craving for tenderness will never be touched unless you offer another woman the sexuality that brings tenderness and love." She tried to out-yell this reasoning by turning up the volume of declaring herself dead to sin. But *since the above three declarations fueled her body of sin (instead of rendering it powerless), she was very much alive to sin.* She had to repent of these declarations and face the likelihood that her hopes for tenderness and cherishing would be disappointed for a long time to come.

On page 66, I gave a general example of a hidden declaration that said, "Your gender is shameful and a dreadful mistake. One false move and you'll reveal the parts of your . . . femininity that you're so ashamed of." The false move that Catherine dreaded was that of allowing men—who had so often failed her—to see that she wanted deep, tender relational involvement. In the past, this window into her soul had been smeared with the foulness of sex-on-demand. To prevent this dangerous window from opening again, she shuttered it with a loud, outgoing, and angry persona that represented the side of her that mocked her femaleness as weak and contemptible. This persona was built on the three distorted declarations mentioned previously. Declaring herself dead to sin, then, had to include declaring herself dead to the destructive lies generated in her own soul.

An overactive conscience is a signal that false guilt and indiscriminate shame are operating deep in the soul. False guilt generates a "truth-system" that competes with the revealed Word of God. The believer wrestling with false guilt actually carries around two sets of "scriptures." One is buried deep inside and consists of such false declarations as Catherine generated to protect her fearful, angry soul. The other is the revealed truth of God in the Bible. The former system interferes deeply with the truth of God. Ultimately, it is traceable to the father of lies himself.

The fact that there is an internal war going on is not the problem. We are clearly told that internal war is part of Christian growth ("For the flesh sets its desire against the Spirit, and the Spirit against the flesh"—Galatians 5:17). The real problem is twofold: (1) We do not recognize part of the real enemy in the internal war (false guilt fueled by early, indiscriminate shame), and (2) this war is being fought in the wrong way as we'll see in the next chapter.

CHAPTER SIX

Fighting One Evil with Another

Do not be overcome by evil, but overcome evil with good. (Romans 12:21)

Do unto others and then run like crazy.
— Old childhood proverb

NOTHING CAN BE more tempting than to believe that to survive in this world you have to give back as good as you get. If you're insulted, come back with a more vicious jibe. If you're cheated, get revenge. If you're rejected, find a way to make them squirm. If your spouse fails you, have an emotional affair (or worse). If your kids make you look ineffective, hit them with the club of dictatorship ("As long as you're under my roof . . .").

When the Apostle Paul says, "Overcome evil with good," two worlds collide. It just seems like common sense that retaliation is the right weapon against being violated. So we keep the club of retaliation handy and do uncomfortable lip-service to Paul's seemingly milquetoast admonition to respond to evil with good.

Somehow, we have decided that Paul (and other pacifists, like Jesus Christ) is promoting a passive, roll-over-and-die response to evil. "Turn the other cheek" becomes a blank check for the wicked to get away with murder. Someday, God will count all the tread marks on our sweet little hides and give us wonderful, shiny crowns to make up for these present injustices.

Such nonsense has more to do with ancient Greek ideas of the inherent evil of matter ("It doesn't matter what you do to me in my nasty, physical body") than with a biblical view of what it means for good to collide with evil. Paul, of all people, collided harshly with evil (rebuking Peter in public was not exactly a wimpy response). His warning in Romans 12:21 is not a call to passivity but a call to examine our hearts as we grapple with evil.

That we *are* to grapple with evil is clear from Romans 12:9, "Let love be without hypocrisy. Abhor what is evil; cling to what is good." These sentences govern the rest of the passage, which ends with 12:21, the verse about overcoming evil with good.

One implication of Paul's reasoning here is that we are to cling to good because it is the thing that overcomes evil. There is nothing passive about this. We are to promote goodness passionately so that we can fling it at evil. Our job, then, is to develop strength in our muscles of goodness so that we can wrestle with evil.

FALSE GUILT AS OVERCOMING EVIL WITH EVIL

The internal war of false guilt against the soul has nothing to do with overcoming evil with good. Instead, it is an attempt to consume one evil with another. The evil of early, indiscriminate shame is attacked by the evil of false guilt expressed through an overactive conscience. The person ends up fighting shame by becoming his own enemy.

For example, one woman put it this way, "I just figure I deserve whatever I get, if it's bad." This twisted belief confirmed the early messages of shame she received, in this case, through sexual abuse. The route of choosing to put herself down caused her to be at war with herself. Self-inflicted wounds are much easier to bear than the call to stand against external evil. As long as she can afflict herself with contempt, she need not face the fact that the real war is against a terrifying evil: that in the heart of her abusive father.

This war against one's own soul is wrong because it is aimed at bringing relief rather than righteousness. Intense, blanketing shame is the acid of early experience that so painfully tempts the person to demand relief. Relief comes first from *accepting* the message of shame ("You are a flaw as a human being") through the operation of false guilt ("Your very presence is an offence"). Then, a person seeks to *cancel* that message through the operation of an overactive conscience (which pushes for impeccable performance).

The preferred campaign of the overactive conscience, then, is to attack one's own soul. The popular name for this self-inflicted pain is a "low self-image" (which strikes me as a synonym for false guilt). Since "it's bad that I'm here," all this person has to offer is impeccable personal performance in response to both internal and external expectations.

Both low self-image (false guilt) and the burden of performance are chosen, cultivated responses to indiscriminate shame. These chosen responses emerge from a shift inside the person. He shifts, in the face of being shamed, from what is a true but vulnerable conclusion ("I have a broken heart, because I am being wrongly shamed") to a conclusion that is untrue but strategically valuable ("I am an ugly and flawed human being"). This shift leads to strategic choices that are painful (low self-image, perfectionism) but protective. It is a shift promoted by a damaged and foolish heart, believing self-sufficiency makes life work rather than dependency on

God. Let's look at the self-sufficiency involved in opting for a low self-image.

FALSE GUILT AND THE IDEA OF A LOW SELF-IMAGE

Most of us think of a low self-image as something that clings to the person, something he would like to get rid of but somehow can't. He would like to believe, for example, that he has something to offer, but his world has told him so many times that he is a nobody, he has begun to believe it. Despite his efforts to think more positively about himself, he just keeps falling into putting himself down. This habit seems built into his personality.

I would propose, however, that the opposite is true. Although a low self-image is painful, *the person* clings to a poor estimate of himself, not the other way around. In fact, a low self-image is basically the same false-guilt, I'm-sorry-I'm-alive strategy that we have been exploring. A low self-image is a cultivated misery. It is miserable because it is truly painful to despise oneself. It is cultivated because it keeps an even more miserable thing under control: the voice of shame. Again, we see that false guilt is used to fight the greater evil of shame.

Don't miss it: False guilt is a form of evil. Why? Because it has nothing to do with a godly sorrow that leads to freedom and passion. Instead, it is a self-focused attempt to protect oneself from a life that hurts and disappoints. Rather than risking rejection from others, rather than hearing them say, in effect, "You're bad," it's easier to beat them to the punch. It's easier to assume, "I'm bad" or "I don't deserve what others seem to have," than to say, "Life is good, but not because I'm particularly attractive or unattractive in and of myself. In reality, the final focus is not me at all but the fact that God loves me. The truth is I'm a mess from head to toe. But God invites me to come to Him. I have no clean evening wear, yet He invites me—smudged, grimy, and impure—to His banquet table. A sumptuous feast is being served, and I am welcome right now. And after I feast to my heart's content, He bids me go out and offer some of His food to others." At this point, any questions about our own attractiveness are simply wrong-headed. Insisting on some reassurance that we are attractive is a subtly cloaked demand to be protected from pain and disappointment. We reason that if we are sleek and shiny enough, others will want us. But then the focus is on us again.

False guilt is, in essence, despair about never being sleek and shiny enough. The overactive conscience that comes from it is a desperate attempt to overcome that despair by sheer effort. Both false guilt and the overactive conscience are wrongly focused on the self. Both are inherently self-centered. Both are easier than becoming dependent on God. Both operate to leave us independent of Him.

PART THREE

WHY DO WE HANG ON TO AN OVERACTIVE CONSCIENCE?

▼ ▼

The Foolish Heart Maneuvers for Independence

THE GOAL OF false guilt is independence. In his heart the person demands to be left alone to resolve the question of the goodness of his own existence with his own resources. He wants to be accepted, but he's so persuaded of his badness that his task seems nearly impossible. He has to be incredibly resourceful to pull it off.

We have looked in depth at one tactic that makes the task of finding acceptance more manageable: that of meeting the expectations of others. This might be called the external mechanism of seeking validity. There is an internal mechanism as well. Like the external one, its intent is to gain validation. Unlike the external one, its audience is not others but God.

THE INTERNAL TASK OF FINDING ACCEPTANCE

The internal mechanism is self-atonement. To the person with a shamed soul it seems that the only hope for neutralizing that shame would be to suffer the pain of inner self-accusation and faultfinding. Self-inflicted punishment is designed to impress God to accept the person in spite of his ugliness.

ı Nathaniel Hawthorne's *The Scarlet Letter*, Arthur ᴅᵢₘₘesdale, having committed adultery with Hester Prynne, secretly and regularly flagellates himself with a cruel whip. Terrified of confessing his sin publicly, he privately exacts a terrible toll on himself:

> In Mr. Dimmesdale's secret closet, under lock and key, there was a bloody scourge. Oftentimes [he] had plied it on his own shoulders, laughing bitterly at himself the while, and smiting so much the more pitilessly because of that bitter laugh. It was his custom, too, as it has been that of many other pious Puritans, to fast—not, however, like them, in order to purify the body . . . but rigorously, and until his knees trembled beneath him, as an act of penance. He kept vigils, likewise, night after night, sometimes in utter darkness; sometimes with a glimmering lamp; and sometimes, viewing his own face in a looking glass, by the most powerful light which he could throw upon it. He thus typified the constant introspection wherewith he tortured, but could not purify, himself.[1]

In his indescribable suffering, Dimmesdale hopes to gain some tiny hope of acceptance from God. But he doesn't know how much suffering to inflict. When will God be satisfied? He doesn't know. He continues to torment himself to the point of exhaustion and sickness.

False guilt is the Arthur Dimmesdale of the soul. Indiscriminate shame has convinced the person's soul that his very existence is tiresome and wrong to others. Even God (or especially God) is offended by the eyesore of the shamed soul. This person anxiously responds by seeking to atone for this "sin." Caustic self-accusation is the primary whip of this self-atonement.

A friend told me of how he felt compelled to stay busy

on his birthday. Weeks ahead of time, he planned a full workday followed by a commitment to take a group of visiting missionaries on a tour of his city that would last far into the evening. By the time his wife asked him if she could plan a party for him, he demurred, saying that his day was full. She was disappointed. He was irritated that she did not understand his "unavoidable" commitments.

Why would a man spend his birthday in overdrive, so crowding his schedule that no one could plan anything special for him? Because, as he put it after some reflection, "Who would really want to give a party for me? I don't deserve one." As we looked into his feeling of being undeserving, he came up with a catalog of self-demeaning images. He saw himself as fat, soft, and effeminate. He pictured himself as disgusting and contemptible, as sort of a sissified, pale slug of a subhuman. Who would want to throw a party for him? With the cruel whip of self-accusation, he beat into submission his longings to be celebrated and loved.

SELF-ATONEMENT:
A MOVE TOWARD INDEPENDENCE

It is crucial to see that the hand holding the whip is one's own. Remember, the goal of false guilt is independence. False guilt is at the heart of a self-governing system that is both autonomous and secret. Exposure is unthinkable. No one (including God) must know the horrors that go on inside. The person must pay, but must also inflict the pain. He never wants to suffer the light of the exposing eyes of someone else, especially God. Because he has never experienced exposure without harshness, he will not believe that God's exposure can be tender and merciful. The person will stay in control of his own suffering. That suffering will be both private and strategic.

I sat recently with a woman whose pain seemed

bottomless. A single mother with two angry, adolescent sons, a manipulative, cruel ex-husband who uses those sons to get at her, a church family that seems to keep her at arm's length, and a demanding job. As we chatted, she came close to tears, but it was as if, on their way to her face, they slammed into a wall and trickled secretly away on the inside. I asked her about the barrier, why it had to be there.

Her mind went to many childhood scenes of loneliness and heartache. Held at a distance by a remote, cold father, she wondered what she had done to turn him against her. And if it was her fault—and she was convinced it was—why was she in such pain? Confused by the ache inside, she punctuated her girlhood with long walks down a rural lane, crying loudly, all alone.

Why, I asked, didn't she bring those powerful tears to her father's attention? She was aghast at my question. "You must be joking," she said with barely controlled disgust. "He would have looked right through me."

"What would that have done to you?"

"I would have felt like a worthless jerk. Like I was stupid for crying. Like I had just told him something vile."

"And if you cry here," I asked, "will I treat you as stupid and vile?"

"I think it's because you're a man that I can't cry in front of you," she said.

"Do you hear the putdown in that?"

"No."

"Because I am a man, I'm condemned by you to be the same as your father."

Her sarcasm was like a lance. "So you want me to cry in front of you, right? That's what will make you happy?"

"What will make me happy is for you to stop putting me in the same corner with your father. I'm trapped there."

"I don't know what you're talking about."

"I'm talking about you putting me in a corner where you can hold me in contempt and neutralize me. You've put me where you don't have to take any risks with me."

This dialogue has a crucial principle at its heart: Whatever this woman is doing with me, she is doing with God. To think that God could be tender and merciful toward her tears is as revolting an idea to her as to think that I could be receptive to them. God, myself, and her father (who deserves to be there) all inhabit the same contemptible corner. The bars of our cage are made of her strong commitment to independence and secrecy. She believes that if she allows us out of the corner, we will prey upon her with our contempt and disgust.

Here, then, is a woman whose suffering is vast but who construes others as predators in order to keep that suffering hidden and under her control. She uses the whip of self-accusation ("You are stupid for crying") to keep her suffering soul sealed in a room for self-atonement. Outwardly, she maintains a "none of your business" demeanor. Inwardly, her suffering is immense, but she is motivated to continue it, driven by the feeling that she must pay. Only by atoning—in a way that is both private and yet is an offering for guilt—can she hope to ward off the feeling that she is utterly condemned.

REMAKING GOD

The audience for all this contempt is God. Here, someone might say, "I thought she was trying to *avoid* God." It is important to see that the God she is avoiding is the God who both sees clearly and loves deeply. This is a combination she longs for (as we all do). Yet she has decided she cannot risk having Him disappoint her, so she remakes Him in the image of an angry disapprover. This is the god who is the audience for her self-atonement. He sits on her shoulder with a critical face and a readiness to scowl. Her life depends on preventing the scowl or, should it darken His face, quickly getting it to clear up.

The effect of this inner treadmill is that she is always inflicting pain in order to avoid pain. She inflicts internal pain (self-disgust) in order to avoid external pain (being exposed and rejected in relationships). She lives in great pain in order to prevent a far greater pain. She develops a lifestyle where it is "normal" to be the recipient of pain.

A person who gets used to self-inflicted pain more easily accepts pain and abuse from others. Those who struggle with an overactive conscience tend to see themselves only as victims. They are the prey; others are the predators. This is a hopeless position. If victimization is all that is true about us, then there is no way out of our pain and foolishness. If, however, we are agents who have chosen a fearful and cynical response to a harsh world, then there is hope. An agent can change. A victim can only suffer.

But change requires trust in Someone outside our self-regulated system. Afraid to hope that the Heart of the universe could be any different than our bitter portion of it, we construe that Heart as untrustworthy and insist on seeing in Him the same caustic accusation we have known so well in our own painful experiences.

Something has come into focus for me over and over as I have worked with people: The foolish heart always maneuvers for independence. This is thoroughly true of the person's heart commitment to a lifestyle of false guilt. Again, false guilt (and the resulting overactive conscience) is a cultivated rather than a fated response. It is a strategic response. It is a chosen response. The degree to which the person can embrace that he is an agent is the degree to which he is close to making another choice entirely, that of risking exposure to a God whose character is radically unlike any he's ever known.

TWO RESPONSES TO THE LOVE OF THE FATHER

But we are stubborn. Suppose this God is only a smooth actor. Suppose He will get us opened and trusting only to pull the rug from beneath us? Maybe we'd better keep Him in the corner we've so painfully constructed for Him.

The story of the prodigal son highlights the ambivalence of the soul vis-à-vis God. Actually, it is the story of two sons: one a repentant prodigal; the other, a disgusted, entitled scrooge. The story begins with the sentence, "A certain man had two sons" (Luke 15:11). We sense that these two are going to be contrasted. And they are. But the younger son dominates the first two-thirds of the story. If we are not careful, we'll read the last third almost as an afterthought. But Jesus' intent in bringing us back to the older brother is contrast, not just rounding off the story. He is teaching us that there are two types of responses to the love of the Father.

Jesus spends most of Luke 15 making an introductory point: God is so loving that He passionately seeks those who are lost. His message is that those who are lost (and there are many ways in which to be lost) have the immediate, passionate attention of their Father. He never reacts indifferently to human "lostness" in any form. He is so passionate to find lost people (and the lost aspects inside His own people), that He is willing to make a fool of Himself.

This idea lands us in the middle of the prodigal son story. There we are told that the father saw his returning son "while he was still a long way off" (verse 20). This suggests that the father remained vigilant for his son's return, even though the son had been foolish and irresponsible. It is even plausible that the story shows a father who scanned the horizon at every opportunity, hoping to see a thing of great joy—the return of his rebel.

What does this father do when his son returns? What

does this horizon-watcher do when the horizon yields a homecoming? Quite simply, he goes crazy. How do we know this? Because the text says, "His father . . . ran." This running is extraordinary. In the culture of Christ's day, older men never, ever ran. Haste was considered self-demeaning, an admission of passion that was unseemly for the wise and aged.

But this father is overwhelmed with joy. He overcomes all inhibition and practically knocks his son down with an extravagant embrace. The text says, literally, that the father "fell on [his son's] neck." And then he "kissed him again and again" (verse 20, NASB margin). Here is a man completely carried away with happiness. In the eyes of his culture, he is playing the fool. He is delirious. The local gossips would be appalled: "The very idea of making such a show over that shabby rebel! Why, if he were my son, I'd teach him a thing or two about making me look foolish in front of the whole town! Rebels deserve discipline, not a sentimental welcome."

It turns out, though, that there are two rebels in the story. Here is where the contrast comes in. Here is where Christ shows the two kinds of responses to the Father's love. We turn from this happy scene, this joyous reunion, to hear the voice of offended propriety. When the older brother finds out what is going on, he is incensed. He refuses to join the party (for now the reunion has become a celebration), so his father goes outside and pleads with him to come in (verse 28).

Listen to the older brother's rationale for his anger: "Look! For so many years I have been serving you, and I have never neglected a command of yours; and yet you have never given me a kid, that I might be merry with my friends; but when this son of yours came, who has devoured your wealth with harlots, you killed the fat-tened calf for him" (verses 29-30). The homecoming and glad reception of the prodigal expose a bitter, demanding heart within the older brother. His motive for serving his father has not been unselfish at all. In fact, he has used his service as a basis for developing a high sense of entitlement. He feels he has some things coming to him as a result of his long service and his compliance with his father's commands.

His bitterness reaches white heat as he spits out, "You have never given me a kid [a young goat], that I might be merry with my friends." Clearly, he has harbored increasing resentment as his sense of being deserving has grown over the years. He has given in order to get. He has been subtly bargaining with his father, trading "doing the right thing" for title to all his father owned.

The father exposes his older son's foolishness when he says, "All that is mine is yours" (verse 31). Amazing! The older son has been trying to earn something that was his all along! Here, his rebellion and cynicism are completely exposed. This son thought his father had a selfish grip on his remaining assets. He would, he thought, have to pry open his father's reluctant fingers, one at a time, through long years of compliant service. After enduring all this servitude, he would be entitled to his father's handing over what the son so richly deserved.

That is why "all that is mine is yours" is so explosive. The son has wasted all that servitude and labor for nothing! He has been toiling to deserve what his father has already graciously relinquished. The older son was too blind to see the character of his father and so lived in a world of unnecessary and selfish pain and sacrifice.

How tempting it is to insist on construing God as mean-spirited and tightfisted. That way, we can labor and toil for Him. This keeps us in control. We call the shots. We keep hidden counsel with ourselves based on our illusions about God's character. Suffering angrily and privately, we continue, as the next chapter shows, to fight off the light of exposure.

▼ ▼

Fighting Off the Light of Exposure

IN CHAPTER 1, I SAID that the overactive conscience is a system for attracting the expectations of others. I compared it to a light bulb on a summer evening, its bright light attracting myriad bugs. By contrast, a light bulb inside a screened porch would still attract bugs, but they would be "filtered" out by the screen.

The diagram on page 90 presents this idea along with the roles of shame, false guilt, and a new concept, functional legalism: As the diagram implies, shame is the trigger that throws this system into operation. Whenever a person feels disapproval, rejection, comparison, or any other threat that comes through his relationship with others, God, or himself, shame—a fear of being exposed for the disgusting creature he sees himself to be—activates a flood of false guilt through the system. False guilt is the "juice," the energy driving the behavior that shame triggers.

This "juice" is powerful. It is a bully. For example, rather than checking to see whether his self-condemnation is realistic, the person simply accepts the intimidating verdict of false guilt: "I am a wretch, and I must hide it and atone for it."

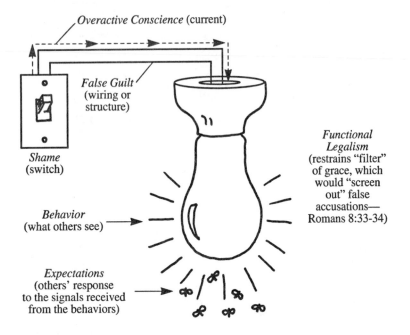

Overactive Conscience (current)

False Guilt (wiring or structure)

Shame (switch)

Behavior (what others see)

Expectations (others' response to the signals received from the behaviors)

Functional Legalism (restrains "filter" of grace, which would "screen out" false accusations—Romans 8:33-34)

But this "current" needs a framework, some "wiring" to give it direction. That framework is provided by the guilt-driven conscience. Every jolt of false guilt is given a focus by the sense of specific deficiency the overactive conscience supplies. The conscience is the container of specific "rules," the breaking of which reveals the clear "deficiencies" of the person.

Here is an example of how shame, false guilt, and the overactive conscience might work together: While on the faculty of a graduate school, I was the last to arrive for a meeting with two colleagues. They were both high-powered and dynamic, accustomed to the "politicking" and influence-peddling that seems to be the lot of many faculties. When I walked into the room, they were seated across from each other near the end of a long conference table. The chair at the head of the table was open. And I also could have sat beside either of them in the next chair down from the head of the table.

I took the seating arrangement in at a glance and immediately suffered an attack of shame. Why? Because to sit beside either of them might offend the other. Worse, I would feel presumptuous sitting at the head of the table. I would be sitting in the "power seat," taking a leadership role with two men I considered quite powerful. This tapped into great shame inside me. I tend to see myself as a "minor leaguer," someone who's never going to make it in the big time. I *want* to be in the "major leagues," and I *sneak* into the big-league games at times; but I have to be careful. I have to pick my spots. You don't just swagger up to the plate and waggle your bat at a major league pitcher when you know, deep down, you're a minor league batter about to be exposed.

Sitting at the head of that table felt like swaggering up to the plate in a World Series game. One second after the shame attack, I felt a jolt of false guilt: "You haven't prepared for this meeting" (there was no preparation to be done); and "You'll get tongue-tied; you won't be able to think on your feet"; and "You're too stupid to keep up with these guys."

My overactive conscience came along and gave these rather vague feelings more focus. The "rules" were: (1) never offend anyone (in this case, by sitting next to one guy without sitting beside the other); and (2) never be presumptuous (by sitting at the head of the table).

Now I must take the story in a fictional direction, since I was able to repent of the false guilt and realize that I was perfectly free to sit wherever I liked. (I sat at the head of the table, by the way.)

But suppose I had been so tyrannized by the false guilt that I was driven by it? Here is what I imagine: I walk in, take in the situation swiftly (my radar for offending others and for my own presumptuousness being finely tuned). My first words would be, "Anyone want coffee?" Then I would turn, go down the hall, get the coffee, and return. During that time span I'd have come up with a solution to the problem of offending someone (the presumption of sitting at the head of the table I would have ruled out immediately). The solution would be to sit down beside the guy closest to the door (that way, I'd have the escape of logic: "I'll just take the nearest seat") and be extra servile toward the guy across from me (to soothe any hurt feelings he might have, just in case). Then, when he runs out of coffee, I'd jump up, go get it for him, and sit down beside *him* when I got back. Voilà! Everybody's happy, and I have lived out my role as a minor leaguer in a major league meeting without risking exposure.

FUNCTIONAL LEGALISM

This, then, is how the triumvirate of shame–false-guilt–overactive conscience works. But there's a new kid on the block. The "new kid" is *functional legalism*. Functional legalism is distinct from doctrinal legalism. Even when we espouse the doctrine of divine grace, we can still function as legalists. In fact, functional legalism has the task of preventing God's grace from working. It serves to prevent grace from setting up a screen to filter out inappropriate, damaging expectations and/or accusations. I call this *functional* legalism simply because the person functions as a legalist, even though he will protest that he believes in God's grace. In reality, he believes he can see God's smile only in the mirror of his own self-effort. Life is built around earning God's acceptance (and that of others) instead of enjoying it.

Mechanical Spirituality

The functional legalist ends up developing a particular kind of spirituality that I'll call "mechanical spirituality." This is an orderly, self-generated spirituality based on the sufficiency of right actions. It insists too heavily on *clarity of standard* rather than moving beyond mere rule-keeping to *compassion of heart*. This is because clarity of standard (e.g., thinking in a black-and-white, do-and-don't fashion) ensures that the rules will be measurable. False guilt demands clear standards because the over-active conscience seeks to resolve the question of personal goodness through one's own resources. Only by establishing my own goodness can I remain independent of God, whom I don't trust. And how can I resolve the question of my own goodness unless I have clear rules to which to conform?

False guilt, then, insists on my being in final control of measuring my spirituality. The resulting mechanical spirituality springs from a fear of putting myself in God's hands. If I can dictate the terms of spirituality, I never have to submit to His wise and thorough exposure of my heart. Why should I? I know how I'm doing. All I need to do is check my clearly measured spiritual standards. Instead of offering God the real pain and rebellion in my heart, I offer Him the false sacrifice of impeccable spiritual performance. The issue, I insist, is not my heart, it is my performance.

This sleight-of-hand that hides the true pain and rebellion in my heart and instead offers the smokescreen of "good" behavior is painfully demonstrated in Luke 18:9-14 —

> He also told this parable to certain ones who trusted in themselves that they were righteous, and viewed others with contempt: "Two men went up into the temple to pray, one a Pharisee, and the other a tax-gatherer. The Pharisee stood and was praying thus to himself, 'God, I thank Thee that I am not like other people: swindlers, unjust, adulterers, or even like this tax-gatherer. I fast twice a week;

I pay tithes of all that I get.' But the tax-gatherer, standing some distance away, was even unwilling to lift up his eyes to heaven, but was beating his breast, saying, 'God, be merciful to me, the sinner!' I tell you, this man went down to his house justified rather than the other; for every one who exalts himself shall be humbled, but he who humbles himself shall be exalted."

The Pharisee is incredibly arrogant. He has the nerve to display his "spiritual" behaviors as if they are the last word on the condition of his heart. He has the audacity to thank God that he is "not like other people." Notice that the accomplishments he cites reflect his insistence on *clarity of standard*. He says, "I fast twice a week; I pay tithes of all that I get." One has the impression that he could go on, that he is selecting only the choicest morsels of spirituality through which to display his advanced maturity.

Why would he want to insist on such a clear but repulsive way to measure his spirituality? Because he demands the right to make an offering to God that costs him nothing. He demands the right to have control over the terms of righteousness. He rejects God's words to Habakkuk, "The righteous will live by his faith" (2:4) and instead insists that the righteous will live by his "performance of carefully displayed deeds."

The Pharisee at the Heart
of the Overactive Conscience

The overactive conscience makes a person a Pharisee. Like a Pharisee, he *wants to be in control of what is pleasing to God*. Why? Because this takes him out of the searchlight of God's exposure. The attitude of the person with a guilt-driven conscience is exactly the opposite of David's in Psalm 139:23-24 — "Search me, O God, and know my heart; try me and know my anxious thoughts; and see if there be any hurtful way in me, and lead me in the everlasting way." David is *asking for exposure*. He desperately wants the searching probe of God's Spirit to alert him to the nasty places in his heart. In this, he is like the tax-gatherer who said, "God, be merciful to me, the sinner." Assuming the ugliness of his own heart, he calls out for mercy. This is to leave the stench of self-satisfied haughtiness and break into the fresh air of humility and brokenness.

THE SEDUCTIVENESS
OF THE OVERACTIVE CONSCIENCE

The overactive conscience, then, promotes pride. The smug Pharisee looks good praying in the temple (just as false guilt looks good by meeting others' expectations), but the real agenda is to cover both the shame and the sin of the hidden heart. The pride is revealed in the person's assumption that he can seduce others into believing his own good opinion of himself. The Pharisee in Luke 18 sought to seduce God into believing that he was "not like other people" by displaying his good works. Similarly, the person with an overactive conscience displays the "good works" of meeting others' expectations. This is done in order to have a reservoir of deeds with which to seduce others into both granting acceptance and ignoring the shame and sin deep inside.

Only by grasping the proud seductiveness of the guilt-driven conscience can we be delivered from the "try harder mentality" that often dominates evangelical views of sanctification. By "try harder mentality," I mean the view that says, "The standards are clear. Our rules of behavior are mapped out for us in Scripture. If we are not attaining them, we need to *try harder*. This includes trying harder to appropriate the strength of the Holy

Spirit, trying harder to act on our position in Christ, and trying harder to carry out the spiritual disciplines." Of course, effort is a part of Christian living, but effort that goes toward establishing a performance to be displayed without exposing a heart that needs both healing and confrontation is useless.

Sanctification, then, cannot be managed by carrying out spiritual disciplines alone. Sanctification is not to be managed in the first place; growth, rather, stems from a grateful response to the mercies of God (see Romans 12:1). Duty is not the primary engine of sanctification; "shoulds" are not the primary engine of sanctification; pressure is not the primary engine of sanctification. Real growth is a matter of "I want to" rather than "I have to." Joy can replace duty as the motivational spring behind spiritual growth. As long as duty remains our primary motivation, we are, as the next chapter shows, harboring a subtle critique of God.

▼ ▼

CHAPTER NINE

False Guilt
as a Subtle Critique of God

A THEME THAT HAS run through the previous chapters is that false guilt is a chosen, cynical response to life's harshness. Now, we need to deepen our understanding of this cynicism. It is important to do so, because much of our cynicism focuses ultimately on the character of God. The overactive conscience is rooted in doubt about the character of God.

Emily was a counselee who felt the constant prod of false guilt. If she walked by someone's cubicle at work without saying hello, she would worry about it the rest of the day: "What if she was hurt? What if she thought I snubbed her?" Then her worry would take a different tack, "If I go back to apologize, what if the person says, 'What are you talking about? I never even saw you walk by.' I'd feel absolutely stupid."

Her tormented mind would work on this and other problems deep into the night so that she could never rest. The next day, she might vigilantly try to read the "offended" party's mood, looking for signs that all was well. But she could never be sure, could she? So the torment continued.

As we chatted about these struggles, Emily began to see them differently. She no longer saw her worry about others feeling snubbed as a way of being kind. Instead, she saw it as her insistence on being in control of how they perceived her. The plan of her heart was to get others to see her in an approving way so that they would never delve deeper to the stained and wounded heart of a woman who had been sexually abused as a little girl. At some point, I asked her, "How do you think God sees your heart?"

What followed was stunning, especially considering that this woman was a believer in Christ. She said, "The idea that God accepts me where I am is just a fairy tale." I offered the thought that a clean heart is not dependent on what happened to her but on what happened to Christ. She dismissed the thought with, "That's a fairy tale, too." The sneer in her voice was heartbreaking. It was as if she had said, "Don't give me that stuff about being washed from sin. I'm as dirty as a prostitute, and no one will *ever* find out. God doesn't have any more ability to accept me than my earthly father who abused me. That's all men are after, anyway. And God is just another man."

What did she mean by "fairy tale"? How could a believer in Christ express such skepticism about the character of God? This cynicism revealed a deep division in her heart. Although she did genuinely believe the gospel, she limited her belief. For her, the good news was only about deliverance, not about transformation. (I suspect that for most who live for the expectations of others, the gospel is not seen as transforming at a deep level.) Of course, she would have *said* that the gospel transforms lives and character, but her actions and attitudes conveyed the real state of her belief: "The gospel delivers me from the penalty of my sin but not from the poverty of my character."

THE MESSAGE IN THE BOTTLE

To get a feel for why this deep division existed in Emily's heart, imagine that she had somehow been washed up on a deserted island.[1] She doesn't know how she got there, she knows only that she is in a dreadful predicament. After a few days exploring the island and finding no phone, no fax, no telegraph, no boat, no food, and no people, she sits on the beach and says, "I'm going to die if I don't find a way out of this predicament."

Just then, she notices something floating in the surf. The sun is reflected as the object washes up almost at her feet. It is a bottle with a note sealed inside. The message says, "There is a rowboat in the next cove under some banana leaves." She jumps to her feet. Could this be real?[2]

She runs to the next cove and, after some searching, finds the rowboat. Her delight soon dissolves into despair, however, for the rowboat is extremely heavy. She can't budge it, even with the strength of desperation. Weeping, she collapses into the sand. Her cheek hits something hard. A sea shell? No, another bottle! Another message! This one says, "Get in the boat, and I'll take care of launching it." She obeys and the boat mysteriously and smoothly moves over the sand, through the surf, and out to sea. She is stunned. What good news! She is delivered.

She drifts for a time, enjoying the unbelievable escape from her predicament. After a while, she begins to be uncomfortable just drifting. She wants direction and momentum. She reaches for the oars and is surprised she can't budge them. They feel as though they're made of granite! Her fingers brush a piece of paper attached to one oar. It says, "These oars are made of wood from the groves of Heaven. You cannot lift them as you are now. To keep drifting, press button one between your feet. To do something about the oar problem, press button two."

Astonished, she looks down. Between her feet—*ta da!*—are two buttons! She hesitates, then presses button two. Nothing happens, except that when she looks up, a man is sitting on the bench across from her about three feet away. She almost falls out of the boat.

"Pardon the sudden entrance," he says, "but you clearly want to do something about rowing."

"Yes," she says, resisting the urge to rub her eyes.

"I sent the messages," says he. "And I've come in response to your prayer."

"I prayed no prayer," she states.

"Any response to me is a prayer."

While she thinks this over, he goes on, "I've come to help you become a rower instead of a drifter."

"Okay," she says. "How do I do that?" She envisions his giving her bigger muscles, putting her on a training program. She imagines weight lifting against progressive resistance, running in place, aerobic sorts of things, vitamin supplements.

Her workout reverie is broken by his next words. "You must sit on my lap and let me put my arms through yours. As you row, I'll be holding the oars with you."

At first she is amazed, then repulsed. Who does he think he is, inviting immediate intimacy? Lap sitting?! How dependent she would be! And vulnerable! She looks down at herself. She is scratched and muddy from days of searching the island in all sorts of weather. Her skin is burned, her lips puffy, her hair scraggly and sandy. She is unwashed. He would smell her if he were that close. *Yuk!*

"How about a weight training program?" she asks faintly, a slight nausea flitting about in her stomach.

"You cannot be a rower with your strength," he says. He is kind but firm. "You must sit with me and be close to me in order to row."

She trembles. He seems to know what he's talking about. He seems gentle. But how could she know? In the past others had seemed trustworthy. Others had seemed gentle. She still bore their scars. Those scars were bitter and somehow fresh. She decides: No more scars. Turning around on her bench, she sits with her back to him. Better to drift than be vulnerable.

She glances over her shoulder. He could be up to something. To her surprise, he hasn't moved. He looks inexpressibly sad. She catches herself being drawn to him, then checks herself coldly. "Anyone can look sad," she tells herself. Crossing her arms, she looks away.

"Be not afraid," he says. She puts her fingers in her ears.

How ridiculous, she thinks. *Sitting on his lap!* A glance at her bedraggled, wet clothes strengthens her resolve. He'd just have to come up with something better. She crosses her arms again.

"I can clean up those clothes for you, if that's the problem," he says.

So that's it, she thinks. Aloud, she says, "What am I supposed to do? Conjure up a tent while you wash my clothes?"

"If you like," he says. "But your nakedness would not be a problem for me."

"Yeah, I'll bet," she says. "Well, it's a problem for me, bub. And you can just forget it."

He becomes silent and sad again. Maybe a bit amused, too, somehow. They drift on in their quiet impasse.

Now let's return to my counselee. Perhaps the division in Emily's soul is a little clearer. She was "in the boat." That is, her *salvation* was not in doubt. But what about allowing the *sanctification* process to touch her stained and wounded femininity? Out of the question! She understood and accepted that the gospel can deliver, but she refused to believe that it can transform.

OUR TENSION ABOUT GOD'S CHARACTER

Obviously, Emily's doubt about the character of God ran deep. And since He was unable (so she insisted) to cleanse her, she had to turn elsewhere to the god of secrecy. Burying it alive, she must keep her stained, wounded, and rebellious heart hidden at all costs. Her secrets must never be told, because opening up in such vulnerability is always (in her view) met with abuse and shame. Even from God. Sit in his lap? Ridiculous!

How was false guilt displayed in her life? Through her obsession with the rule that everyone must perceive her in an approving way. She *must* say hello to everyone so she didn't lose ground in her campaign for approval. If that campaign didn't win her enough "votes," she'd be rejected. Then her guilt and shame would be confirmed: "See, you deserved to be abused. And now everyone knows it." Her guilt, of course, was false. No one deserves to be abused, especially not for being female. But try to tell her that. She held tenaciously to the false guilt as an incentive to hide her femininity and to "make up for it" by being an asset to everyone around her.

The false guilt that fueled her overactive conscience sprang in turn from the strategy of doubting God's character. With God written off, she could operate on the assumption that all she had to offer others was a dutiful performance, the purpose of which was to control how others saw her. Like the Pharisee in Luke 18, she was out to seduce others into accepting the little she had to offer and thus to miss the real chaos in her heart.

Like the Pharisee, too, she accepted the "try harder" idea that she should be in control of her own growth and acceptability. She did so through the seduction of well-performed, but empty duty. Others were given the role of applauding her dutifulness and refusing to seek out her shattered heart.

SEDUCED INTO ACCEPTING CRUMBS FROM ONE ANOTHER

There is a crucial theme here: The person with an overactive conscience seduces others to be satisfied with a minimum offer of herself. Like the woman in the row-boat, she wants others to accept that she has turned her back—that is, that she will not permit intimacy. Unlike the man in the rowboat, who wants the woman to offer more, others usually take us up on this avoiding of intimacy, because they, too, shrink back from it.

Most of us, especially those with excessive false guilt, have our backs to each other, relationally speaking (this is true, as well, for most marriages). But shunning real intimacy brings deep tension. It is harder to get people to like you from a distance, and people with an overactive conscience insist on being liked. So we must foster the illusion of intimacy, painting a "smiley face" on the back that we present to one another. The "smiley face" usually comes in the form of impeccable performance and ingratiating niceness.

There is a cynical seduction in the idea that others will be taken in by the "smiley face," naively mistaking it for real intimacy. The overactive conscience convinces us that others are fool enough to be duped easily into accepting superficial contact in place of real relationship.

But others do not fall for the smiley face because they are stupid, rather they fall for it because they want to have their own smiley face accepted. It is a *mutual* scam! But no one exposes it, because intimacy is a too-dangerous alternative. Thus, we conspire in an "under the table" agreement to defraud one another. Many relationships, then, are a reciprocal seduction and really not relationships at all but arrangements. They are arrangements of mutual seduction: "You accept my smiley face, and I'll accept yours." Or, "You be satisfied with relational crumbs, and I will, too." The person driven by false guilt is especially insistent that this be true.

Here, too, is a key idea. The overactive conscience motivates us to look scrupulous and "moral." But, since we accomplish this mission through seduction, it cannot be truly moral. Though our actions may look scrupulous, the drive behind them is seductive. Being motivated by false guilt, then, is not equal to being concerned with righteousness but with conspiracy, which is rooted in cynicism both about God and about others. This picture of the immorality behind the overactive conscience emerges strongly in the next chapter.

CHAPTER TEN

What the Overactive Conscience and the Seared Conscience Have in Common

IN THE OPENING VERSE of 1 Timothy 4, the Apostle Paul has an explicit message from the Spirit of God that "in later times some will fall away from the faith." Not only will they pay attention to "deceitful spirits and doctrines of demons," they will also be "seared in their own conscience as with a branding iron" (1 Timothy 4:2).

THE SEARED CONSCIENCE: A TRIUMPH OF SELF-DECEPTION

What does it mean to have a "seared conscience"? We get a clue from Paul's comparison of the seared conscience to the operation of a branding iron. The heat of the branding iron cauterized the skin, killing the nerves in it and rendering them useless. Anything that entered the skin after branding would not be felt. That portion of the skin could no longer function as a warning center for maintaining the integrity of the body. The lifeless flesh could not alert the body to impending danger.

In the same way, the seared conscience, because something deadening has been applied to it, no longer functions as a moral warning center. The deadening agent that has been applied to it is "the hypocrisy of liars" (4:2). That is, some had listened to lies and had answered their screaming consciences with those lies for so long that those consciences, far from screaming, no longer even whispered. Just as intense heat sears the skin, so repeated falsehood sears the conscience. A seared conscience is evidence of the triumph of internal falsehood.

If applied falsehood is the first feature of a seared conscience, the second is that it can go dead in one of two directions: license or legalism. The former is what people usually think of as evidence of a seared conscience. When I read in the papers about serial killers or rapists, I immediately think of them as men with a seared conscience. The fact that the license in them to kill or harm is so complete indicates that the conscience is completely lifeless.

But what about the legalist, the man or woman who operates under the watchful eye of false guilt? Could this, too, be evidence of a seared conscience? Can a legalist with an overactive conscience be, on some level, just as deadened as a serial killer? To explore this, we need to turn back to Paul's letter to Timothy. Having described those who will "fall away from the faith" as having been "seared in their own conscience as with a branding iron" (1 Timothy 4:2), Paul goes on to describe, not license, as we might expect, but legalism. Those with a seared conscience are "men who forbid marriage and advocate abstaining from foods, which God has created to be gratefully shared in by those who believe and know the truth" (4:3). Clearly, in this case, the seared conscience tends toward legalism. There is not, in fact, an iota of licentiousness in this whole passage. Paul is alarmed by the legalistic fruit of the seared conscience. In other places (e.g., the Corinthian letters), he is upset by license. But here, the heart of God's apostle is inflamed by those who would limit legitimate Christian freedoms. And he makes it clear that these illicit limits are the illegitimate offspring of a seared conscience.

And he has more to say on this subject: "for bodily discipline is only of little profit" (4:8). I think this refers to asceticism ("bodily discipline")—the idea that the body is inherently evil and needs to be brought to submission by denying it all enjoyment. He says to avoid asceticism, because "godliness is profitable for all things" (4:8). Thus, Paul finds the evidence of a seared conscience, not in license (although that is shown to be true elsewhere, see Titus 1:15-16), but in the making of restrictions that deny men and women the enjoyments God intended for them (this is the essence of legalism) and in the practice of asceticism.

The conscience becomes dead, as we've seen, by the repeated application of falsehood. When that falsehood takes the form of portraying God as a cosmic killjoy who shudders when any of His children are having fun, the conscience then becomes seared in the direction of legalism.

It is no mere coincidence that, when Satan desired to tempt Eve into disobedience, he pictured God as withholding something good: "You surely shall not die! For God knows that in the day you eat from it your eyes will be opened, and you will be like God, knowing good and evil" (Genesis 3:4-5). Satan hotly challenged the goodness of God's character. He pictured God as a petty, childish tyrant who would be really chapped if Eve discovered she could have one of His toys. Satan's attack on God's character implied that He is a Grinch who can't stand to open His hands and *really* give generously. "Ha!" said Satan. "The Divine Tightwad won't even let you have a piece of fruit without threatening death. He's getting severe only because He's afraid you'll find out what's really available to you."

The thief of all thieves and the liar of all liars dared to portray God as tightfisted! Our God who created the universe and made us His servant-rulers over it and who gave beyond the utmost in sending His own Son from Heaven to die for our sins was made to look like a cheapskate! God, the most openhanded Being of all, was lampooned as a threatened, miserly scrooge!

Does this leave you incredulous? Does it make you angry? It should!

No wonder, Paul alludes to "deceitful spirits and doctrines of demons" (1 Timothy 4:1). It is certainly a demonic doctrine that represents God as down on marriage and as putting all kinds of restrictions on the foods His children may eat (verse 3). Indeed, a seared conscience cannot discern these lies that spring from Satan's agenda to call God's character constantly into question. The seared conscience, then, remains dead under the monstrous, repeated falsehood that God is a selfish miser, that God is a taker and not a giver.

OUR FEAR THAT GOD IS A TAKER

If God is a taker, then what are we to do? We must become takers, too, living on whatever we can wrest from Him and others. We take whatever we can and pour it down the black hole of our voracious self, trying to fill ourselves up. We must get what we can and hold on to it at all costs. We must protect the assets we have painfully garnered for ourselves. And we must get more!

Here, our insides are exposed for what is really there: a gnawing emptiness that expresses its hunger by grasping and pulling on the meager resources available in a fallen, sinful world. After all, if Satan were right, and God really is withholding, shouldn't we resort to getting all we can? If there is a closed hand at the center of the universe, then shouldn't we grab the few crumbs that might still remain? Isn't this what God-the-miser is modeling, anyway? And doesn't His closed hand prove that it is a shame that each of us is alive as another hungry mouth, another competitor for limited resources in a gloomy universe?

I talk to so many people who remember parents with closed hands and closed hearts, and they are tempted to believe that God is withholding, too. In so believing, they, like their parents, become acquisitive, trying to fill the black hole inside with the scant emotional resources they can wrestle away from others. But they carry a guilty secret inside: "My inner ache is so gnawing I can hardly stand it. The great pain just proves that I am greedy. How can anyone who wants and aches so intensely be anything but a parasite? I must hide both my ache and what I am doing to feed it."

This fits right in with messages of indiscriminate shame such as "You're a disappointment," "You're in the way," "You were our mistake," "I wanted a boy, not a girl," "We found you in the garbage," "Why do you have to be so clumsy?" and on and on. Such shame makes it impossible to feel the ache of wanting to be filled without at the same time concluding that it proves how bad we are. The fact that we are voracious just proves, we think, how utterly shameful we are.

THE LIE OF SHAME

So, when our conscience, still trying to function well, says, "It's okay for you to want to be loved," we throw this lie at it: "You're just greedy and selfish. How dare you want anything! You're lucky to be allowed on the planet." The voice of shame lies viciously to the conscience. After enough of these caustic lies, the conscience no longer speaks up in defense of our real design. It becomes seared by falsehood. We begin increasingly to deny our design. We ignore the precious clue that lies in the midst of our voracious, grasping soul: *If we followed our inner ache where it really leads, we would discover that we are starving for God!*

Far from being a source of shame, our inner hunger

is a signpost pointing out our need for God! How does the Bible respond to this hunger? "Everything created by God is good, and nothing is to be rejected, if it is received with gratitude; for it is sanctified by means of the word of God and prayer" (1 Timothy 4:4-5). What are we to do with our hunger? Satisfy it! God's storehouse is open to us: It is good to feast on whatever God has given as long as it is received with gratitude. Why the condition of gratitude? Because thanksgiving acknowledges that the feast is nourishing only when we recognize that it comes from the hand of God. What are we to do with our hunger? Eat well, and thank God!

Here, the healthy conscience says, "It's okay to acknowledge your design." The seared conscience, on the other hand, remains deadened by the lie that hunger is only a shameful proof of weakness and selfishness.

The overactive conscience, then, is ironically another species of seared conscience. Why? Because its aim is to hide our shame over our hunger and emptiness. Instead of acknowledging these as evidence of our design as image-bearers, it requires us to steal emotional crumbs from others. Instead of bringing our hunger out in the open and acknowledging what it really is (a soul starving for God), it requires us to be thieves, using the crowbar of impeccable performance to pry open the hands of others. Forcing them open, we grab crumbs of approval, affirmation, and belonging.

The seared conscience, then, does not always lead to a departure into license. It can also lead to a departure into legalism. *The purpose of legalism is that of hiding our hunger, because we are ashamed of it. We must both control it by not wanting anything and secretly satisfy it by stealing emotional crumbs from others who applaud our dutiful performance.* But what *must not* happen is for anyone to see our aching soul. That would bring the death-dealing voice of shame that says, "You're such a pain. Can't you do anything right? Why can't you be like the others?" If the conscience applies this lie to itself often enough, it will eventually die, becoming unable to warn about the evil of denying one's design (or that of others). At this point the conscience is seared.

THE FORK IN THE ROAD

The seared conscience puts the person on a bad road with a bad fork in it. The bad road is that of denying his design. The bad fork is that of choosing either license or legalism:

THE "FORK" OF LICENSE	THE "FORK" OF LEGALISM
1. "Doesn't matter what I do"	1. "What I do matters completely"
2. Others are merely targets	2. Others are merely resources
3. Classic sociopath	3. Subtle sociopath
4. The god of appetite	4. The god of performance

Note that *both* forks in the road lead to a sociopathic (conscienceless) position: One believes that people are targets for satisfying the god of appetite; the other sees people as resources for satisfying the god of performance. And *both* forks lead to a conscience that is deadened to the presence of evil. Because the legalist has no depth-knowledge of evil, he does not sense the fact that he is using other people.

No matter which fork is taken, the tragedy of the seared conscience is that it removes a warrior from the army of righteousness. A warrior cannot fight an enemy he doesn't recognize. The seared conscience ensures that evil will not be recognized and that it will not be confronted at its root. No wonder Thoreau said, "For every thousand who are hacking away at the leaves of evil, there is one hacking at the root." For example, the more someone denies his own design, the more likely it is that he will deny the design of those around him. The more he denies their design, the more he uses them. And because he denies his design, he doesn't *feel* himself using them. Because they also deny their design, they don't feel the violation of their souls. And so the molesting of human souls goes unrecognized. *The seared conscience never reports it.*

Thus, even believers go about ineffectually hacking at the leaves of evil ("I never allowed my daughter to go to a prom") while missing the root of evil in the molesting of a human soul ("I used my daughter to make me look good as a Christian even as I refused to give her my heart"). Incidentally, when the molesting of a human soul goes on with impunity, the molesting of the body cannot be far behind. The absolute mushrooming of sexual abuse (both in the committing and reporting of it) has its precursor in our culture's (including the church's) turning a blind eye to the widespread molesting of the human soul. How can the body be safe from attack when the soul is molested with impunity? How can the body be safe when relationships so often mask the covert assault of the inner being?

Why is the Apostle Paul so determined to point out the "fork" of legalism? Because he knows that legalism conceals cynicism about God's character and carries the seeds of permission to take advantage of others. Legalism violates the two greatest commands: Love God, and love people. Legalism is built on the foundation of hating God (because He is seen as cheap and selfish) and hating people (because the person feels justified, in light of God's bad character, in stealing from them emotionally).

OUR HATRED OF GOD

Now we are at a frightening place, the place of seeing that a guilt-driven conscience is not merely noble overzealousness. It is not simply a bad habit. It is not an inborn temperament or trait. A guilt-driven conscience arises from a secret greed to fill my own soul on my own terms. I insist on my own terms because I do not trust God to touch my hunger. In fact, I hate Him for His closed hand and His hard heart. I will build my own barns and storehouses out of boards stolen from others, and I will feed greedily in them rather than bring my empty, longing soul to Him whom my soul hates for His failing me.

This is the frightening place for the person with a seared conscience: I hate God because He has failed me, and now I am on my own. If I'm going to find enough crumbs to fill my soul, I'll have to do it with my own ingenuity. But, deep down, I know I have bitten off more than I can chew. I'm stuck between the rock of filling myself and the hard place of impotence. I've insisted on guaranteeing my own fullness, but I know, in some deep place, that I'm impotent to pull it off. This is a frightening position. I've demanded a job I can't do, but I can't admit that to anyone. I can't even fully acknowledge it to myself.

THE TERRIFYING DILEMMA

This impossible dilemma—not being able to do the job and not being able to acknowledge—makes us crazy. This double bind is the source of our nonorganic symptoms and struggles. We feel the dilemma deeply in our souls if we stop to think and feel deeply enough. But it is so terrifying that we usually don't stop long enough to sense it. In fact, most of our busyness and most of our routine, auto-pilot lifestyle is *designed* to prevent our feeling this dilemma.

Let's look at the dilemma more closely through the story of Sally, a thirty-ish Christian woman with three children, a husband, and an active, demanding lifestyle. Sally grew up in a home where criticism was the air she breathed. Her father—the source of most of the criticism—constantly invaded her fragile boundaries with thrusts of accusation and faultfinding. Once, he screamed at her for not cleaning the *underside* of the toilet tank sufficiently. Another time, he jerked her out of her room in front of a playmate, scolding her harshly for leaving a broom against the wall after dutifully sweeping the kitchen.

Her father became to her an ogre whose face was always filled with lines of anger and blame. She began to feel overwhelmed by the assaults. Life soon revolved around trying to quiet the ogre. The best strategy, she reasoned, was simply to perform flawlessly. Even though she saw herself as deeply and irreparably flawed, she determined never to let him see that. She must cover it up by performing perfectly: *Always* put the broom up, *always* make the bathroom transcendently spotless, *always* practice the piano, even on Saturday, but *never* bother your father with the noise.

Now the dilemma begins: Sally must guarantee her own well-being, but she could not absolutely maintain the perfection that ensures it. One slip and the ogre would wake up and assault her soul with acrid contempt. Only the shield of perfection could stand against his arrows of disgust. But what if her shield had holes in it? Her solution was very simple: *There would be no holes.* To think otherwise, to allow the slightest relaxing, would be to risk the acid of disgust. More disgust, she felt, would quite simply kill her.

This commitment was successfully maintained until Sally got married. Now, she found herself brought once again into closeness with a man. She panicked inside. What if she couldn't maintain her perfection under this close scrutiny? She feared desperately lest her shield be pierced and her soul wither under disgust from her husband.

This new panic had the good effect of causing her to come to Christ for the first time. She was born anew and found a measure of peace. But there was a fly in the ointment: Because Sally still saw the world as a place where acid lurked and where her heart was always in desperate peril, she simply saw God as another weapon in her distorted struggle for perfection. Rather than allowing God to be the Father who would be delighted with her, Sally insisted that He help her run a flawless life that would protect her from the ogre she now carried inside.

When God didn't help life run perfectly, she was incredulous. "Why won't God help me?" she asked. "Why won't He cooperate in giving me a world that runs smoothly? Is that too much to ask? What kind of God would not give His child this small thing?" She begged God for parking places that would allow her to be on time. She pleaded with Him for kids who would not drop food on the kitchen floor. She wrangled with Him for light traffic so she wouldn't be late for car pool. When He didn't provide these things, she flew into a rage. These small things she asked for—how could He deny them?

Sally didn't realize that these were not "small things." Far from it! Asking for these things *was equivalent to asking God to sanctify her greed for perfection.* Two things can be said about this greed. First, her greed sprang from her insistence on resolving her dilemma (guaranteeing her well-being without being able to guarantee the perfection that would establish it) in her own strength and ingenuity. Second, as Colossians 3:5 explains, greed is simply a form of idolatry. That passage lists some things we should be dead to. Among them is "greed, which amounts to idolatry." The original language is even stronger in that it says "greed, which is idolatry." Greed, in whatever form it takes, boils down to idolatry.

Sally's greed for perfection was idolatrous. In asking God for perfect circumstances, *she was asking Him to help her carry out her idolatry.* In one counseling session, I said to her, "Sally, God is not going to subsidize your idolatry. He is not going to help you start a fire on an altar you have set up in opposition to Him."

These words highlighted her dilemma. Without her idolatry for perfection, she had only one alternative: to risk letting the ogre spew poisonous disgust all over her exposed soul and to trust that God would somehow be there to love her. She shuddered at the prospect. This felt like certain death to her. She would rather be goaded toward miserable perfection by false guilt than to trust in God's character.

HOW TO RESOLVE THE DILEMMA

No wonder we hesitate to look at our dilemma, at the hollow ache inside. No wonder we have become so skilled at living on auto-pilot. No wonder we prefer the cattle prod of false guilt to the abyss of trusting God in the valley of the shadow of death. How do we move *toward* our dilemma rather than away? How do we overcome the whip of a guilt-driven conscience?

Three things need to happen to free us from false guilt: (1) We must have a way to tell the difference between those things we should feel guilty over and those we should not. In other words, what needs atonement and what doesn't? (2) We must develop the capacity to accept that some things about us as individuals *are* bad. And the things that are bad have been taken care of at the cross of Christ. We must accept this, too. And we must learn to accept and relax into these things so deeply that we can be truly *thankful* for them. (3) In the relaxing glow of thankfulness, we need to learn freedom. Thankfulness throws off the shackles of necessity. Freedom completes the emancipation by moving us further from necessity as a motivational system and toward worship as a motivational system. These three joyful companions—*Christ's atonement, thankfulness,* and *freedom*—will join us on the path that is both the good fork in the road and the rest of this book.

PART FOUR

▼

How Do We Move Away from an Overactive Conscience?

▼ ▼

CHAPTER ELEVEN

Embracing Christ's Atonement Rather Than Our Own

RICK WAS A COLLEGE STUDENT who came for counseling because of academic problems. He simply wasn't keeping up with his studies even though his intellect was superior and his motivation high. As we chatted, it emerged that he approached all reading assignments almost with a sense of nausea. Seeing the enormous amount of reading to be done in a semester, he would begin to read each night with a commitment to cover a lot of ground. As he read, though, another feeling crept over him. What if he were reading *too* fast? What if he were not conscientiously getting the nuances of the textbook? What if he were rushing through the sentences faster than the professor would consider appropriate?

So, he asked the professors about it. But they were no help. They always said the same thing: "Read as fast as you need to but not so fast that you don't get the basic content." Well, what is "basic content"? Is there some un-basic content? How do you tell? Obviously, Rick was over-scrupulous. But he could not stop. By the time he came for counseling, he was hopelessly behind and terribly frustrated.

It was apparent to me that Rick's scrupulousness was

motivated by false guilt. He was, to use the language of this book, voracious for expectations. In some ways, he was comfortable in the university because there were many expectations to fulfill. But when the expectations became unclear (what is "basic content"?), he got incredibly frustrated. The expectations were there, but he wasn't sure how to meet them. Yet he *had* to meet them in order to have the affirmation he required.

His desperation for affirmation was, in part, traceable to an elementary schoolteacher who responded to his childhood asthma with stern discipline. Assuming that his asthma was a manipulative attempt to deal with his unfounded insecurities, she simply ignored the milder asthma attacks and disapprovingly sent him home with his mother if the attack was more severe.

Because of the teacher's attitude toward him he felt ashamed of his special need. He responded by trying to meet her expectations in all other areas. He hoped to build up a fund of goodwill in her that might divert her contempt for him when an attack came. While he prayed that he would have asthma symptoms only at home, he also prayed that—if symptoms occurred at school—his teacher would be distracted from her contempt by his previous hard work at being perfect. His absolute rule: Don't be deficient anywhere else.

ATONE OR DIE

Thus, at the university, Rick was terrified that his professors would find his work deficient, because *perfection was the only way he had to atone for the "deficiency" of having asthma.* Another principle emerged: Without atonement, he could expect only the same death-dealing disgust he had felt in elementary school. Atone or die. These were his choices.

But this cycle—atone or die—is not something only

Rick experienced. It is a cycle that is woven into the very fabric of the way things work. Since an offended deity inhabits the control center of the universe, we know we must either atone or die. Hebrews 9:22 puts it clearly: "without shedding of blood there is no forgiveness." Of course, if there is no forgiveness of sin, there is only one result: death (see Romans 6:23). There it is: atone or die.

Rick's struggle, then, simply clarifies our own. His offended deity is an elementary schoolteacher; his sin is that of having asthma. But the outcome is the same for all of us: atone or die. While the dilemma—atone or die—is universal, it raises an enormous question: Atone for what?

The Bible is crystal clear about it. Atonement is always aimed at *sin*. Sin is any attitude, belief, or action that constitutes rebellion against or transgression of God's character. Any such rebellion or transgression must bring either atonement or death.

But the sinner is in a predicament: Atonement must be made by one with clean hands. In other words, the sinner cannot cleanse himself. Someone must do it for him. Further, since "without shedding of blood there is no forgiveness," whoever makes atonement must die. And the death, to atone effectively, must be the death of one with clean hands.

Of course, only Christ meets this description. He is the only One with clean hands. He is the only One who could die in an atoning way. The dilemma that we all face—atone or die—was met by His agreement to die for us so that, once we receive the benefits of His death, we no longer face that dilemma at all. The Christian is *off* the treadmill of trying to make atonement in order not to die (of course, self-generated atonement is futile anyway; attempts at self-atonement emerge from Satan's lie that God can be replaced).

PUTTING THE OVERACTIVE CONSCIENCE
OUT OF BUSINESS

Accepting Christ's atonement is true not only for relationship with God but, by extension, for all relationships. Rick, for example, needed to grasp that final atonement had been made. And since the greater deity, God, has been satisfied by the death of Christ, it follows that all lesser "deities"—such as the elementary schoolteacher—must be seen in the same light, that is, that no further atonement is necessary. The result is that the overactive conscience is now outmoded, since it is rooted in the atone-or-die dilemma that has been resolved in Christ's atonement. When Christ said, "It is finished," He was referring to Rick's feeling that he had to do something about what was wrong with him. Rick was correct in sensing that something was wrong with him. But he was wrong in concluding that he could fix it.

Rick was also wrong about something else. While the news about atonement is stunningly good, it gets even better when we return to the question, "Atonement for what?" As we've seen, the Bible clearly says that the aim of atonement is *sin*. Christ's work pays sin's penalty. The payment is made in full. Something wonderful follows: What is wrong with each of us has to do with sin, not with being human. None of us has to atone for being human. Rick's humanity included a vulnerability to asthma. He is not wrong to have asthma. He does not have to atone for nonsinful shortcomings, no matter what another person's attitude about them may be.

HOW WE MAKE THE GOOD NEWS SO BLAND

Yet the issue of atonement is precisely where our mental and spiritual fog is the thickest. Most Christians are not at rest over this issue, especially those driven by an overactive conscience. In fact, self-atonement is the core of false guilt. Why are we so unaffected by the very gospel we believe for salvation? Why doesn't the gospel bring us the rest we can begin to experience this side of Heaven?

Indiscriminate Shame

I believe the culprits are two: (1) indiscriminate shame and (2) our stubborn propensity to doubt the character of God. Let's camp again on the idea of indiscriminate shame for a bit.

As we discussed earlier, we carry a pair of components in our human makeup: dignity and depravity. The "dignity component" prompts us to ask the question, "Am I loved?" Because we are made in God's image, we simply long for unconditional love. We cannot rest until we find it any more than we can soothe thirst without a drink. We are restless for love.

But we are also rebels. Our "depravity component" stirs us to ask, "Can I get my own way?" An energy inside us yearns to sit at the pinnacle and call the shots. We are restless to find a way to be the captain of our own ship. We have a restlessness for selfish gratification.

Now, imagine a child who, like all of us, carries around these two components, and let this simple diagram represent the child:

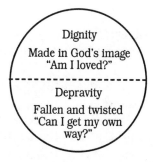

Dignity
Made in God's image
"Am I loved?"

Depravity
Fallen and twisted
"Can I get my own way?"

The child brings these two components into every interaction. His parents, for example, encounter a thirsty fool in their conversation with him. The thirst stems from his dignity; the foolishness from his depravity. Parents rightly respond to the depravity in the child by trying to provoke sorrow in him over his foolishness. Every instance of discipline should create an atmosphere in which the child feels sorrow over sin. This sorrow over sin is what I would call legitimate shame.[1]

Now, our diagram might look like this:

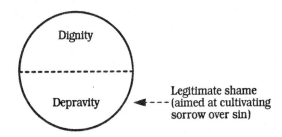

So far, so good. Shame is doing what it's supposed to: getting foolishness to wither away. But follow me for a moment into the mind of a parent who (like most of us) does not have a handle on the realities inside his child. Moreover, he does not have a handle on the realities inside *himself*. All he knows is that he is tired and his kid wants something from him.

Consider the following exchange between a child and his father, who is preoccupied with the newspaper.

CHILD: Dad, I want to play with you.
FATHER: Just a minute.
CHILD (after a moment or two): Dad, I really want to play with you. Can we play catch outside?
FATHER (not looking up): We'll see.
CHILD: When? Soon? I want to play *now*!

FATHER (exasperated): Will you stop being such
    a pest!
CHILD (hurt): You never play with me.
FATHER (stung and enraged): Do you have to make
    a federal case out of this? Leave me alone! Go
    play with your sister and get out of here!

Does the child have a legitimate need to play with his
father? Yes. Does the father have a legitimate need for
relaxing after a hard day at work? Yes. Who expresses his
need more clearly? The child. What does the father do?
Rather than admitting his need and trying to work out a
solution, he applies shame to what was never meant to
bear shame—i.e., the child's need for love as expressed in
a desire to play with his father. Shame's withering power
is directed at the child's dignity, his longing for love. The
child is tempted to feel shame over that longing: "I am bad
for wanting my dad to play with me."

Our diagram now reflects this component of illegitimate shame:

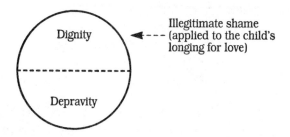

Dignity

Depravity

Illegitimate shame
(applied to the child's
longing for love)

False Guilt Takes Root
Rather than feeling good about wanting to play with Dad,
the child begins to doubt that this is okay. If these sce-
narios continue, the child will become convinced that his
wanting to play with Dad reveals something shameful

about his character. He begins to feel flawed as a human being, that something is dreadfully wrong with him for wanting Dad's time and attention. He begins to hide his needs (which he now feels are shameful) behind a tough exterior. Underneath, he feels both angry at his dad and wrong for needing anything from him.

The weeds of shame over his neediness begin to sprout. He tries to keep the weeds under control with the machete of false guilt: "If I can do enough things right, I can control this and no one will know how bad and weak I am." The performance-oriented lifestyle is a way of hacking at the weeds that grow in the soil of illegitimate shame.

Here is where the good news about Christ's atonement becomes doubly liberating. The child in our discussion is no more wrong for wanting his dad to play with him than Rick was wrong for having asthma. Thus, when we ask the question, "Atonement for what?" we can again refine it by asking, "What is wrong with me?"

Now we can see that we must not answer that question while under the influence of illegitimate shame. When we think about what is wrong with us, we must think in the direction of personal depravity, not in the direction of our dignity. We are not wrong to want to be loved. How we go about seeking love is another issue, but our desire for love reflects our design to be loved. We can no more ignore our design for love than we can ignore the nose on our face. Both are part of each of us as individuals. What is wrong with you and me? Is it the fact that we long for love? Well, is it wrong that we each have a nose?

The Good News Is Radically Good!

Once we come to these realizations, the good news of the gospel comes more clearly into focus. What is wrong with you and me? We are sinners, both by constitution and practice. But there is a remedy, a final solution in the atoning death of Christ. What is wrong with you and me? It is *not* that we are human. It is *not* that, in our human, God-given dignity, we long for love. It is *not* that, in our humanity, we will have imperfections, including sicknesses like asthma.

The atonement of Christ does three things we desperately need: (1) It confirms that something is wrong with each of us; (2) it clarifies what is wrong (sin); and (3) it completely mends what is wrong with us.

MORE ON DOUBTING THE CHARACTER OF GOD

As we reject the influence of illegitimate shame, we will be more able to enjoy and celebrate our liberation and our Liberator. But a second culprit trips us up in our journey out of illegitimate shame: our stubborn doubt about the character of God. To understand this more fully, let's go back to our diagram:

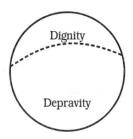

Note that, over time, the person's sense of the "okayness" of his dignity has withered almost entirely. He has only a few safe places wherein he can come alive and enjoy being made in God's image.

Perhaps when he is alone in his car and a good song comes on the radio, he finds himself singing his heart out and beating time on the steering wheel. When he comes to a stoplight where others might see him, he stops singing and swaying to the music. Those minutes alone on the open road might be the only time in the course of an entire week or month that he is aware of a passionate aliveness in his soul. This is because he has developed a way of thinking about his life that is protective rather than passionate. His aliveness is a well-kept secret behind barriers of soul-numbing thought-patterns.

Our diagram now depicts these barriers as follows:

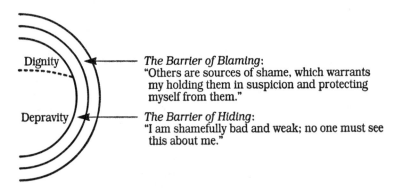

The barrier of hiding has, in effect, been discussed in our exploration of illegitimate shame. Illegitimate shame "confirms" that we are "bad and weak." The second cul-prit—our doubt about God's character—emerges from the barrier of blame. The first use of blame as a barrier is quite ancient. In fact, it can be seen in Adam's response to God in Genesis 3:12—"The man said, 'The woman whom Thou gavest to be with me, she gave me from the tree, and I ate.'"

This is staggering, both for Adam's audacity and for what his response says about all of us. In the heart of human beings is a stubborn commitment to avoid respon-sibility by blaming God. Adam does this in two ways. First, and most obvious, he attributes his sin to the fact that God gave him this troublesome woman: "the woman whom Thou gavest me." Second and more subtle, Adam pairs the two acts of giving: "The woman whom Thou *gavest* me, she *gave* me from the tree" (emphasis added). Adam ungratefully links Eve's sinful giving of the fruit to God's gracious giving of Eve. One is a gift, the other a betrayal; but Adam lumps them together. Not only are we willing to blame God, we do so by distorting His character. In our mania to avoid responsibility, we make God the whipping-boy for our struggles.

Adam opens Pandora's box when he has been warned against it and then blames God for his failure. This despite the fact that God, knowing of Adam's disobedience, comes to Adam, not to destroy him, but to ask leading questions that point to a doorway of grace. Adam turns his back on grace and clings to the brazen move of blaming God's divine character for his own self-inflicted wound.

Our Earthly Fathers and Our Distrust of God

Most of us think we have distorted God's character because of our tendency to see Him through the spectacles of others' character flaws and how they have hurt us. For example, it is a modern truism to say that Rick, for example, cannot trust God because he cannot trust his own earthly father. The platitude is that we see God in a distorted way because others have failed us. And while Rick's view of God may be influenced by the relationship he had with his father, Rick does not distort God's character *because* of that relationship.

The tragic response of Adam to God shows that it takes no prior, cruel paradigm to get us to distort God. Rather, we distort God because it is convenient to our rebellious purposes to do so. *How* we distort God *may* be influenced by prior relationships, but the *fact* that we distort God is due to our own depravity.

Now we must sophisticate our diagram a bit more:

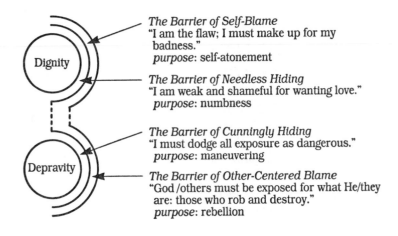

The Barrier of Self-Blame
"I am the flaw; I must make up for my badness."
purpose: self-atonement

The Barrier of Needless Hiding
"I am weak and shameful for wanting love."
purpose: numbness

The Barrier of Cunningly Hiding
"I must dodge all exposure as dangerous."
purpose: maneuvering

The Barrier of Other-Centered Blame
"God /others must be exposed for what He/they are: those who rob and destroy."
purpose: rebellion

Simply put, we hide two things that shouldn't be hidden: our longing for love and our demand to be captain of our own ship. Similarly, we blame in two directions: toward what reflects our contempt for ourselves and toward what reflects our contempt for God and others.

The gospel of Christ completely disrupts this system. By dying for our sins, Jesus destroys the idea that our problem is our humanity and places the blame squarely on our depravity. The problem, He implies, is not that we are human but that we are subhuman. We have fallen far from what it means to be human, but we have an inkling of what it means in the fact that children want to play with their fathers.

Christ makes it equally clear that we do have a problem, and His atonement makes no room for cunning or for other-centered blame. His work throws a floodlight on our scheming and our subsequent campaign to smear God's character. The good news releases us to enjoy our humanity and develop it into what it was designed to be: Christlikeness. And the good news is radically bad news for our attempts to maneuver and rebel.

The gospel, then, is both an invitation and an attack.

It is an invitation that allows the blossoming of our long-ing to be loved. It is an invitation to explore our design and bring it to maturity and fruitfulness. On the other hand, the gospel is an attack on a rebellious stronghold. It is an attack that exhausts and withers our prideful maneuvering.

The gospel holds up a mirror that, in effect, is bifocal. In one part we see a delightful picture of who each of us was meant to be: Christlikeness expressed through a unique personality. In the other part, we see who we have become: subhuman, prideful rebels who, anxious and arrogant, assume the prerogatives of God. If we see this rebellious picture clearly, we must either superim-pose on it the cross of Christ or be destroyed by our conscience. Perhaps this is why we falsely transfer the strictness of conscience to the first, delightful picture, seeking to feel falsely guilty over the unique design God has given us. We drag our design rather than our deprav-ity into the spotlight of judgment. In this way, we avoid the shock of seeing how bad our depravity really is. That is, our doubts about God's character include doubts about the adequacy of Christ's sacrifice on the cross. In order to avoid putting the cross to the test (what if it doesn't pass?), we transfer our guilt and shame to the part of us that reflects the design and image of God.

The cross forces us to see that our guilt should revolve, not around our design, but around our devious persist-ence in asking, "Can I get my own way?" We find that we have both less and more to be guilty about than we thought. Our guilt is lessened with regard to our design. We are delightfully freed to pursue who God has made us to be. But our guilt is increased with regard to our rebel-lion. We see more clearly the leprosy in our own souls and our conscience is filled with reproach.

The joy of seeing that we are not on the hook for our design is offset by the anguish of seeing that we *are* on the hook for our sin. Our leprosy is so advanced that, when we see it clearly, the sting of conscience is excruciating. The pain is so great that we are immobilized. How can so great a leper heal himself? Where is he to turn? Our immobilization is unbearable until we see it for what it is: a chance to be still and see that the cross is the collision of wrath and mercy.[2] In that collision we are able to make out the gift of forgiveness. The leper has a place to turn! He can be made clean!

Now we see clearly. No longer do we need the foolishness of self-atonement (foolish in that it attacked our design and masked our sin) that is at the heart of the guilt-driven conscience.

CHAPTER TWELVE

Moving Away from an Overactive Conscience by Cultivating Thankfulness

It came about while He [Jesus] was on the way to
Jerusalem, that He was passing between Samaria
and Galilee. And as He entered a certain village,
there met Him ten leprous men, who stood at a distance; and they raised their voices, saying, "Jesus,
Master, have mercy on us!" And when He saw them,
He said to them, "Go and show yourselves to the
priests." And it came about that as they were going,
they were cleansed.

    Now one of them, when he saw that he had
been healed, turned back, glorifying God with
a loud voice, and he fell on his face at His feet,
giving thanks to Him. And he was a Samaritan.
And Jesus answered and said, "Were there not
ten cleansed? But the nine—where are they? Were
none found who turned back to give glory to God,
except this foreigner?" And He said to him, "Rise,
and go your way; your faith has made you well."
(Luke 17:11-19)

LEPERS WERE THE AIDS-carriers of ancient cultures. They
were considered to harbor a malady that could explode

in society, decimating the population and wrecking the stability of social structures. As such, they were considered unhealable, unapproachable, and were to remain unassimilated. Forced to live in quarantined colonies, they formed lonely, miserable communities of their own. Lepers lived lives of enforced alienation. By the laws of Israel, they had to cry out, "Unclean! Unclean!" whenever they came near the healthy population. This cry was a warning to the healthy that danger was near.

The leper was a walking contagion, a living stigma. Unwanted, feared, and loathed, the leper was completely identified—both in his own mind and in that of the surrounding culture—with his disease. He was a *leper*, not a human being who happened to have leprosy. Today, this would be like calling someone with cancer a "cancer" or someone with AIDS a "virus." In ancient cultures, those with leprosy were completely shut out. In a private, earthly purgatory, they communed only with those who were mirrors of their own misery.

OUR SPIRITUAL LEPROSY

Leprosy is a near-perfect metaphor for the condition of the sinner. Apart from the work of Christ, sinners are unholy and unclean in the sight of God. Since unholiness stains righteousness and cannot associate with it, the unholy have no choice—apart from the gospel—but to be banished into a quarantine. The biblical word for this quarantine is *hell*. Hell is the place where unholiness can exist without infiltrating the holy. Here, the analogy breaks down in that leprosy is not a moral issue, but sin is. If sin were allowed to intermingle with righteousness eternally, there would never be a place where God could "wipe away every tear from their eyes" and where "there shall no longer be any death; there shall no longer be any mourning, or crying, or pain" (Revelation 21:4).

Hence, God does not hate sin because of some insecurity on His part (e.g., the idea that God hates sin because He is a cosmic spoilsport) but because sin, by its nature, always ruins the haven that God has made for man. Hell is God's way of saying, "If sin insists on existing, then let it exist where it cannot ruin My plans to give My people a haven."

Thus, while leprosy is not a moral issue, it is a good picture of the lack of rest in the life of the sinner. Loathed and full of corrupting flesh, the leper has no place to turn. Using the metaphor of leprosy, let's see how an overactive conscience adds to the wretchedness of the sinner.

Lepers Were Considered Incurable

In the Bible *leprosy* is a term for a number of diseases, some more severe than others. But the common denominator for all of them was hopelessness. There was no reliable way to interrupt the course of the disease, and most lepers eventually died of the infections to which they were so vulnerable. A miracle was the only hope for the leper, and in Israel, the rabbis considered the healing of a leper as difficult as resurrecting the dead.

Consider being reduced to such a hopeless condition. Any activity you undertake as a leper is, on one level, equivalent to rearranging the deck chairs on the sinking Titanic, pointless and futile. On top of that, the surrounding culture sees you as a bacillus, a holder of infection, a container of catastrophe. Like nuclear waste, your "storage" is sternly regulated, your isolation complete. Unlike nuclear waste, there is no "radioactive decay" period for the leper, no gradual fading of toxicity. The condition is permanent. The curse is lifelong. As a leper you cannot be healed.

Imagine the following vignette in which a group of three lepers are marking time in a bar within their miserable colony:

LEPER 1: What do you guys want to do tonight?

LEPER 2: Like we have so many options.

LEPER 3: Right. Want to go to a movie?
(Other two lepers laugh sardonically.)

LEPER 2: Yeah. And leave a finger in someone's popcorn like last time?

LEPER 3: You really shouldn't push yourself on people like that!

LEPER 2: I guess you're right. Maybe I should just give them a piece of my mind.

LEPER 3: I'm sure one will fall off soon. (Yuk, yuk.)

LEPER 1: C'mon, let's get serious.

LEPER 2: We've gone beyond serious to grim.

LEPER 3: Okay. How 'bout this? We could go to town and scare children.

LEPER 1: You know we're not allowed in town.

LEPER 2: You mean if we were, you'd go scare the kids?!

LEPER 1: Knock it off, moron.

LEPER 3: That should be easy enough!

The black humor in this dialogue is, of course, purposeful. Darkness and humor combine when one is striving to squelch a pain beyond endurance—not a physical but an emotional pain. Black humor bubbles up out of tears. One forces the humor out of his mouth just ahead of the tears in his eyes. But the hot tears invade the humor and forge in it a streak of unexpected grimness. The laughter hides a wail. The leper cannot be healed.

The physician, Luke, was not, however, writing in a medical journal. He did not write his gospel to advance our knowledge of leprosy. It is our knowledge of the human condition that he wrote about. Leprosy is a mirror that reveals the true state of my soul and yours. It is ugly and "unhealable." All of us really are, on a deep level, a bacillus that carries a terrifying plague. At strategic moments, our depraved soul spills forth its contents and destroys. Relationships become sites of infection as we career through life saying, "What is wrong with me?" but being unable to prevent the wrongness from being expressed (see Romans 7:18-19).

As I write this, I'm not blind to the fact that I am also made in the image of God. But since my depravity is total, it affects everything about me, including my willingness and ability to express the fact that I bear God's image.

Prior to Christ's coming into a person's life, then, he or she is a leper, unable to be healed. In spite of a nagging feeling that something is terribly wrong and that he is terribly in its grip, somehow he cannot stir himself to be any different. The leprosy of sin continues to infect others. Their leprosy infects him. He is both sinned against and sinning.

The Intrusion of the Cross into Our Leprosy

Now let's observe another dialogue. Two unusually honest friends are sharing a table in a bar. Deep in their cups, they begin to talk freely, initially in a reflective way:

> FIRST MAN: What do you want to do after we leave here?
> SECOND MAN: I dunno. Not go to another bar. I'm getting too old for bar-hopping.
> FIRST MAN: Too old. Hmmmm. That's scary.
> SECOND MAN: But true.
> FIRST: What do you want to do then? Make it go away?
> SECOND: Yeah. But I can't figure out how.
> FIRST: How 'bout another beer?
> SECOND: That won't work.
> FIRST: Okay. Mr. Morose, so we're getting older. What're ya gonna do?
> SECOND: I guess I could do something a little more

grown up.

FIRST: Like what?

SECOND: Stop fooling around.

FIRST: Fooling around! You?! Well . . . hey, that's not so bad. Keeps the juices flowing. Your wife doesn't know, and you know I won't tell.

SECOND: You'd *better* not.

FIRST: I won't. Besides, I do a little fooling around myself.

SECOND: I sort of knew that. But it's not the same.

FIRST: What's not the same?

SECOND: My fooling around and yours.

FIRST: That's ridiculous. Fooling around is fooling around.

SECOND: Not when it's with your own daughter.

FIRST: (after a hesitant gasp) That's gross. Your daughter! That's horrible. She's only nine years old.

SECOND: Oh. You mean it would be okay if she was sixteen?

FIRST: Don't get sarcastic with me, you lowlife. I can't believe you!

SECOND: Oh, you're so high and mighty all of a sudden, Mr. Adulterer. I know who you're fooling around with—your wife's best friend.

FIRST: (another gasp) How'd you know that?

SECOND: Everybody knows who's got eyes. You two were practically all over each other at that bar on Third Street last week.

FIRST: Who told you that?

SECOND: Friends. Your stench is everywhere.

FIRST: Stench?! Talk about a stench! You're abusing your daughter and *I've* got a stench?!

SECOND: What's the difference?

FIRST: It's your own daughter!

SECOND: It's your own wife you're playing for a fool.

Again, what's the difference?

FIRST: Don't try to drag me down to your level, you scum.

SECOND: Yeah. You and I. Pondscum in the lake of hell. I'll see you there.

The first man utters an obscenity and staggers out of the bar. The second stares stonily into his beer, his right fist clenched so that his fingernails dig crescents into his palm. The friends never see each other again, their relationship breached by a new birth of the leprosy. One leper infects his daughter. The other infects his wife. As they struggle to break free, they infect each other. The leper cannot be healed. Every attempt to get out of the colony results only in the annexing of new territory. The colony is everywhere. There is no way out.

This is symbolized in Luke's account by the fact that Jesus meets the ten lepers at the entrance to a village. We are not told the name of the village because the point is this: Anywhere that is clean is out of bounds for the leper. The ten lepers are *outside* the gates to the clean place, the village. They can't go in, because the clean place would become infected. They carry the colony everywhere. The leper cannot be healed; the sinner ruins everything he touches.

Outside the gates, Jesus hears these ten lepers crying out to Him for mercy. And He heals them. With a few words, He completely redirects their lives. Now, we must completely change the dark forecast. Light breaks in! No longer is the leper unhealable! Rather, the leper is healed when the Lifegiver washes away his deadness. In the same way, the sinner is cleansed when the Lifegiver, the Water of Life, washes him or her. All the filth, all the corruption is put away in the sight of God. Things are so new they can be described only as being born all over again. What does it mean to be new in this way?

Imagine that our man in the bar gradually unclenches his fist. His anger sobers him into new reflection. He pays his bill and steps out of the bar, heading nowhere in particular. Adrift on a sea of emotion, he is somehow borne along until he finds a set of stairs to sink down on. His mind is turbulent. Nothing is clear. Images of his daughter compete with pictures of himself as a child.

He hugs his knees. Something to hug. *That's all I wanted*, he thinks. The tears of the leper begin to come. He is afraid of them. Black humor tempts him; he forces a grim smile and thinks, *I guess I hugged her, all right.* Then he sees her face. For the first time, he looks in her face. She is afraid, compliant, and blank. This is not the place for humor. He is haunted by her face, hunted by her blankness. The humor dries up and the tears threaten.

But without humor and sarcasm, there will be pain. *I can't stand the pain,* he thinks. He panics. He is lost again in the sea of pain. This time there seems to be a whirlpool that will suck him down forever. He goes from panic to the brink of an unspeakable horror. At the edge of the suction, at the brink of the watery abyss, he looks frantically for something to hang on to.

Looking up, he sees a cross. He laughs suddenly. "This is just like a story," he says. The sarcasm makes another attempt. "Wouldn't you know? A sure enough *deus ex machina*. A coward's way out." He almost grabs the ladder of sarcasm to numb his soul to the pain. But his daughter's face looms out at him. To climb that ladder is to deepen the blankness in her face. The ladder is both his survival and her death. "It's me or her," he tells himself. "Well, who ever gave me anything?" His heart begins to shrink. He reaches for the escape ladder and feels the abyss begin to weaken its suction.

In the wind and noise of his mind, a welter of images continues to jostle. The cross, his daughter's face, the stone in his heart. But he can clearly see the ladder and his hand reaching for it. Even a leprous hand is strong enough to reach for escape. Yet somehow he is being forced back, jostled away. Somehow—it must be the wind—the cross has cracked and fallen toward him. Just as his hand closes on the first rung of the ladder, the cross impales him. Instinctively, he grabs it and falls, writhing, into the abyss.

The wind blows where it will and drives the cross into the heart and hands of those who, by nature, don't want it. The man in the story has already decided against his own daughter. His fear of his own pain entrenches his selfishness, and he is willing to go on being an agent of death to her. So, the cross comes crashing in purely as an operation of mercy. He had already decided against it.

I am reminded of a story with a similar twist. At the end of Flannery O'Connor's "The Artificial Nigger," this wonderful passage occurs in which one of the main characters, Mr. Head, has sinned deeply against his own grandson:

> Mr. Head stood very still and felt the action of mercy touch him again but this time he knew that there were no words in the world that could name it. He understood that it grew out of agony, which is not denied to any man. . . .
>
> He understood it [mercy] was all a man could carry into death to give his Maker and he suddenly burned with shame that he had so little of it to take with him. He stood appalled, judging himself with the thoroughness of God, while the action of mercy covered his pride like a flame and consumed it. He had never thought himself a great sinner before but he saw now that his true depravity had been hidden from him lest it cause him despair. He realized that he was forgiven for sins from the beginning of time,

when he had conceived in his own heart the sin of Adam, until the present, when he had denied poor Nelson. He saw that no sin was too monstrous for him to claim as his own, and since God loved in proportion as He forgave, he felt ready at that instant to enter Paradise.[1]

The flame in O'Connor's story and the abyss in ours are the same thing. They are operations both of judgment and of mercy that expose the sinner thoroughly and then embrace his embarrassing nakedness with a cloak of a "righteousness not [his] own" (Philippians 3:9). Exposed and embraced, the sinner enters the village! That is, the sinner, embraced by Mercy in all his exposed ugliness, is clean. He can now move into closeness and intimacy. His starving soul has a place, *a Person* in whom to dwell intimately. "Abide in Me," says Christ. Draw near!

This is what it means to be new: no more isolation, no more tears, no more dark humor.

In the amazing newness of this moment, one thankful leper turns back, finds Jesus (who has probably gone *into* the village by this time), and falls at His feet. Aside from his own kind, it is the first time in years this man has come close to another human being. In verse 12, the ten lepers had been standing "at a distance." But now, this healed leper is at the feet of Jesus. *He comes close to his Deliverer and gives thanks.*

The Energy of Thankfulness
Versus the Energy of the Overactive Conscience

Thankfulness is the opposite of the energy that drives an overactive conscience. The overactive conscience reflects a drive that comes from a person's belief that deliverance comes from his own frantic efforts to perform, that unless he performs impeccably he does not belong anywhere, and that since there is no rest from this performance illusion, there is no time or place for thankfulness.

On the other hand, the leper who returns to Jesus reflects an entirely different drive: he comes close to his Deliverer and gives thanks. There are three radically cleansing winds blowing through his soul.

First, *he believes there is a Deliverer.* This is a radical wind for two reasons: (1) the Deliverer is the One against whom he has rebelled, and now he finds himself dependent on Him, who was his sworn enemy; (2) a contrary wind blows in our secular culture, one that stems from secularism's contention that no God will save us, each person must save himself.

To believe there is a Deliverer, then, *our life as a rebel must end.* We must lay down our weapons and bow the knee to our Master. One main weapon in the rebel arsenal is, as we have seen, false guilt. The guilt-driven conscience is simply another ladder out of the abyss of trusting God in the midst of pain. As we saw in chapters 9 and 10, such a conscience is built on cynicism about God's character. We are angry at Him for His failure to cooperate with our idolatrous attempts at perfect performance.

To illustrate this angry, demanding attitude, suppose the ten lepers, as they cry out for help, envision Christ responding by turning everyone else in the village into lepers. Wouldn't that solve their problem? Then they could go in and out of society, blend in anywhere, and have the freedom they long for. How foolish! How pointless to choose an option that costs everyone his health rather than the option—trusting Christ for healing—that restores the lepers to health.

Yet this is exactly what an overactive conscience wants! The guilt-driven conscience operates under the assumption that, *since we are willing to be prostitutes, everyone else must be willing to be a customer.* Before you close this book, please remember that the Bible often resorts to graphic language to make a point. Now, let me explain the metaphor. Motivated by false guilt we prostitute ourselves in that we offer ourselves slavishly to meet the expectations of others in exchange for crumbs of approval that we pretend are real love. Others "pay" us for meeting their expectations. They pay us with these crumbs of approval. It is an arrangement that has nothing to do with real relationship, nothing to do with the giving and receiving of love.

Says author Alan Jones,

> Human beings are trivialized and reduced by hidden assumptions and definitions that render them of no consequence. In an age when nearly everything is disposable, human relationships are understood as just another item in a consumer society. We enjoy or abuse each other as long as we "get" something out of the relationship. Our friends, allies, and partners are disposable and interchangeable.[2]

The overactive conscience, then, proceeds out of a horrible, cynical metaphor. In this metaphor, all we can offer are our "services" of being driven and bound by the expectation of others. And others simply become our customers, throwing us a few crumbs for our efforts. It is a user/used system, a predator/prey arrangement. Unlike the usual predator, others "pay" us for our cooperation. We are angry at God that others do not cooperate, do not "pay" us reliably. We are angry that others do not become lepers with us.

Does this sound too strong? I don't think it is. Is this any stronger than saying, "Their throat is an open grave, with their tongues they keep deceiving, the poison of asps is under their lips, whose mouth is full of cursing and bitterness, their feet are swift to shed blood, destruction and misery are in their paths" (Romans 3:13-16)? Paul's words are aimed at both Jew and Gentile (verse 9). That is, all humanity falls under this description. Biblical language never hesitates to drive home the seriousness of our condition.

False guilt is a refusal to take our condition seriously. It is a manifestation of the inborn, fallen trait of insisting that God can be replaced. It is a rebel stronghold. Posing as a noble hyper-conscientiousness, it conceals a mutineer. As such, it stands directly in the way of our developing a thankful heart. A usurper is not thankful toward the king whose throne he has stolen.

Yet, when we grasp—and are grasped by—the jolting thought that atonement has been made (chapter 11) and that we are cleansed (this chapter) and brought near to Someone who both pays a price for us and tracks us down to offer us the gift He has purchased for us, our eyes are opened to the Deliverer. The secret shame at the heart of our guilt-driven conscience is now washed away! The chains of self-disgust begin to fall away! *Freedom becomes thinkable* as we hold the hand of the Deliverer and walk with Him.

But there is another consideration, an external one (the first was that we are rebels by nature). This one is generated by the secularized culture all around us. Irvin Yalom, in *Existential Psychotherapy*, distills this current into its essence when he implies that belief in God as the ultimate Rescuer is an "anthropocentric delusion."[3] In other words, to believe in an ultimate rescuer, a message in the bottle, is to buy into a pitiful fiction because we can't stand the thought of the universe being meaningless and empty. Many voices in Western culture have fed this stream of thought until it has become a raging torrent, flooding our culture with despair and leaving everywhere the debris of lives shattered by our Herculean attempts to become our own deliverer. The human frame is too fragile to bear the weight of being its own rescuer. The more our own well-being depends on us, the more we groan under the weight of a task that is beyond us. Yet where are we to turn if there is no Deliverer?

The guilt-driven conscience has a ready answer: The only route to well-being is to perform perfectly, to be an unfailing asset to others. Never, never, never disappoint anyone. Never, never, never be a liability. When this internal stream runs into the culture-wide river of secularism—which says, there is nowhere else to turn—it is amplified enormously.

The end of our career as rebels, then, depends on repenting of the energy behind our overactive conscience and then swimming out of the secular torrent that roars with the voice of despair, "There is nowhere to turn, except to yourself." We desperately need a foundation for both repentance and exiting secular despair. The foundation is this: *There is a Deliverer.*

The Deliverer invites us to draw near. A second cleansing wind engulfs the leper. He comes close to his Deliverer and gives thanks. He believes not only that there is a Deliverer but that He invites us to come close to Him. Jesus does not love us through rubber gloves and a surgical mask from behind a bank of computerized microsurgery gadgets. No, He gets us in a bear hug and loves us with the white-hot radiance of His presence. He is the Friend who sticks closer than a brother.

Luke 5:12-13 gives a stunning illustration of Jesus' willingness to touch the unlovely:

> It came about that while He was in one of the cities, behold, there was a man full of leprosy; and when he saw Jesus, he fell on his face and implored Him, saying, "Lord, if You are willing, You can make me clean." And He stretched out His hand, and touched him, saying, "I am willing; be cleansed." And immediately the leprosy left him.

Jesus touches a leper. And not only that, He touches "a man *full of leprosy*," Luke's phrase for the fact that his was an advanced case.[4] This was no grand-standing act. This was no selective contact—i.e., touching a leper with a mild case to keep His risk at the minimum and yet build His reputation. Jesus was touching a man whose case of leprosy had developed to be as bad as can be imagined.

The point is as clear as it is stunning: Jesus is not put off by any ugliness in the sinner. He is able to face whatever is inside each of us. He will never use distance or disgust in His relationship with us. He invites you and me to come close to Him, no matter what we are bringing with us.

Most of us think, "People will like me only to the extent that they don't really know me." I hear this often from counselees. Recently, a woman who is very active in a Christian organization told me, "I simply can't imagine telling my story to my friends in church or the Bible study. They all seem to have grown up in perfect homes with white picket fences." I assured her that she was only sensing that because others' facades were working as well as her own. But her point was well taken: The church is not usually a place where we are invited to know and be known deeply. I suspect that most evangelical church services are massive exercises in self-control (not the kind that is the fruit of the Spirit, either). The self-control is spurred by this conviction: "Anyone who really knew me would reject me."

Jesus, though, is cut from a completely different cloth. He says, "Come to Me, all who are weary and heavy-laden" (Matthew 11:28). What is it that makes us weary and loaded down? Among other things, it is the knowledge of our own shame. It is the burden of our glaring flaws and the contempt they could trigger in others. Jesus, however, invites us to come *with* all the things that are wearisome to our souls, including our past, including our present, including all the things we would shudder to let anyone else know.

The Deliverer welcomes our thankfulness. What do I do, given that Someone has invited me near and has cleansed me completely? The response of the leper is deceptively simple. "He fell on his face at His feet, giving thanks to Him. And he was a Samaritan" (Luke 17:16). Thanksgiving is simple in that gratefulness is such an instinctive response to unexpected and delightful gifts. It is *deceptively* simple in that there are so many barriers to thanksgiving. The barriers are great as shown by the fact that only one of the ten healed lepers returned to thank Jesus for His gift of wholeness.

What are the barriers that hinder our giving thanks to God for His indescribable gifts? Luke gave us a hint when he pointed out that the thankful leper was a Samaritan. Why do we get this tidbit? The Samaritans were, at times, used as counterpoints to the smug self-righteousness of the chosen people, the Jews. One need only think of the story of the good Samaritan (Luke 10:25-37) to recognize that Luke enjoyed puncturing the bubble of smugness that comes when blessings are taken for granted. The Jews were, at times, a picture of the complacency that springs from awarding merit badges to oneself.

Of course, the guilt-driven conscience thrives on such self-congratulation. Desperate for praise, it often provides its own. It is amazing how self-abasement and arrogance exist side by side in the same heart. The person who insists he is *uniquely* undeserving often feels deeply deserving of credit for the astuteness of his own self-loathing. Because he has beaten everyone else to the punch, he gets angry when others do not encourage him. "I know I'm bad," he says. "I've already punished myself for it. Now it's about time somebody recognized that good deed."

If others don't come through with praise, the overactive

conscience will then permit self-congratulation (after all, the whole point of developing an overactive conscience is to gain affirmation). The self-congratulation is most clear in the attitude of the Pharisee we've already gotten to know in Luke 18:11-12—"I thank Thee that I am not like other people. . . . I fast twice a week; I pay tithes of all that I get." The overactive conscience provides a mirror set in a handle made of self-effort. In that mirror, we gaze at the reflection of our own merit, and we congratulate ourselves. And all blessings tend to be seen as further indications that we are, on the whole, fairly commendable (underneath this, of course, is the self-loathing that shame engenders). God's blessings are used merely to polish the mirror of self-effort and increase our sense of self-congratulation.

The greatest barrier to thankfulness is self-congratulation built on the feeble prop of personal success in living up to others' expectations. Sometimes I wonder why thankfulness to God is not more natural to me. I wonder, "Am I thankless toward God because I am so used to directing my thanks and praise toward myself?" As I reflect on this, I draw the sad conclusion that, in order to bolster my insecurity, I often whisper my own anxious praises into my ear. When I don't get a response from others, I fall into the habit of providing my own response. In this response, I either inflate myself unrealistically, or I put the other person down. This is my way of assuring myself that I *have* lived up to the expectations of others, that I am a card-carrying asset to everyone who crosses my path, even if they haven't had the sense to see it. Many people with an overactive conscience react the same way.

The more I become engrossed in this relational calculus, the more I focus on filling my own emotional tank with self-praise. This leaves little room for directing my thanks toward God. I am so busy making sure I'm okay, I forget that He has assured me that my well-being is complete. Having missed His point, I anxiously peer into the mirror of my overactive conscience, looking for warts and pimples, terrified of wrinkles, and critical of my too-heavy eyebrows or my sagging jawline. Every day requires a massive emotional facelift as I anxiously pump self-congratulation into my own ego to make up for gaps in the affirmation that others have insultingly failed to give me. Caught up in this desperate patching up of my own soul, how can I give thanks to Him who has made it well with my soul?

Each of us must come to Him as did the lepers and cry out, "Jesus, Master, have mercy on me!" He responds to such faith not by saying, "Go, show yourselves to the priests," as He did to the lepers, but by saying, "Go, look in the mirror." He does not, of course, mean the mirror of an overactive conscience but the mirror of His own love and forgiveness. There, we see that our soul is clean and whole. As we look closely, we see that the mirror is made of the eyes of God. This is how He sees us! In His sight we are fresh and flourishing, completely restored.

Earlier, I said that the rabbis believed that healing a leper was as difficult as raising the dead. Now I understand that on a deeper level. As I look in the mirror of God's eyes, I see that something has indeed died and something else has come to life. My old self has died. I don't have to keep resurrecting it by injecting the competing "scriptures" of my own self-contempt. If I choose to do so, I must recognize that self-contempt is chosen and cultivated by me in order to resurrect my old self so that I can be in control of my world.

More and more, I see how foolish this is, especially in light of the fact that something has, indeed, come to life. I am forgiven. Thus, I am cleansed of my old foulness (2 Corinthians 5:17). I *am* a new creation. Something new *has* come to life. In God's eyes, I peer closely and see a reborn soul, spotless and unblemished. And I am thankful to Him. The leper comes to the Deliverer and gives thanks. Except I am not the leper anymore. That is why I give thanks.

The burden of this chapter has been to use the picture of leprosy to say that some things about us *are* bad. In fact, we are born sinners. There is nothing we do more naturally than sin prior to coming to Christ. Our instinctive feeling that something is wrong with us turns out to be right on target. But what we discover as we look at Christ cleansing the leper is this: What is wrong with us is what God says is wrong. An implication of this is that we should not allow others' shaming of us for legitimate longings to determine our sense of what is wrong with us.

It is worth repeating the emphasis at the end of chapter 11: *We are not on the hook for our design.* We are not on the hook for deeply yearning for a world in which we are unconditionally loved and in which we make a significant, eternal impact.

Now I am doubly thankful. I am thankful for Christ's cleansing me by dying on the cross to heal my leprous condition. Further, I am thankful that *it is okay that God designed me for relationships that give both a sense of deep love and profound impact.* And while I am never guaranteed that I will receive those things consistently in this life, I am able (with God's help) always to choose to *give* those things in this life. In so doing, I recognize both my design and that of others, whether they choose to recognize mine or not.

Is this not something of what Christ meant when He said, "Love one another as I have loved you" (John 13:34)? The kind of love that Christ gave was self-giving, unilateral, and sacrificial. From Him, we learn that love is never to be seen as a demanded reciprocity. Rather, love is more like a unilateral adventure. Alan Jones puts it well: "One of the hardest transitions to make in the life of faith is that from loving someone for our own sake and loving someone for his or her own."[5] Like most adventures, loving for the other's sake can be painful and dangerous (and thus it is not to be romanticized) but also exhilarating and challenging. Most of all, it is an adventure that is full of freedom.

THE LINK BETWEEN THANKFULNESS AND FREEDOM

Thankfulness, then, is the middle phase of a journey into freedom. The first phase involved resting in Christ's atonement rather than depending on our own efforts at atoning. This middle phase has been a wrestling with the issues of thankfulness and the things that prevent thankfulness as ex-lepers. Clearly there is an inexorable link between thankfulness and freedom.

Let's spell out that link. If our "food and drink" consist of living up to the expectations of others, then we are enslaved to getting a response from others. But we can't *guarantee* that we will get that response. Yet it is our *food and drink* to get that response—that is, it is a matter of life and death. We *must* get the response from others that tells us we are approved and valid. If we don't get that response, it is as if we can't breathe.

When we are living like this, we have no freedom. We are motivated solely by necessity, by what we have to accomplish. It doesn't matter whether we want to or not, we must get a certain level of approval from others. Only approval and affirmation can keep the acid of shame from engulfing our soul. Whenever our "approval-tank" drops below a certain level, we feel the approach of shame. As shame increases, we get more and more urgent about getting approval. The diagram on page 153 might help us visualize the relationship between loss of approval and the intensifying of shame.

Let's see how this diagram works out in the way we

live. Dan was in a homosexual triangle for ten years. Living with two other men, he was the odd man out most of the time when the two paired off. But when they sensed Dan turning elsewhere for relationship, they would break ranks for a time and include him in their parties, their drugs, and their sexual intimacies. Dan would temporarily feel accepted. In other words, Dan lived for the crumbs that the other two men would throw him when they sensed their power over him was waning.

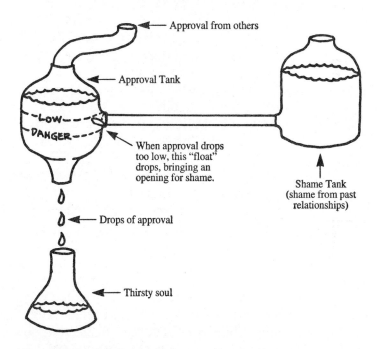

I asked Dan, "Why were you willing to be kept dangling in that relationship for ten years?" His reply was tragic and chilling. "They were the only ones I thought would ever give me anything." Of course, these two predators were not *giving* Dan anything in the real sense of that word. They threw him crumbs to manipulate him back

into their orbit so that they could hold him in contempt
from the fortress of their own sick pairing.

As Dan and I sought the roots of his distorted belief
that crumbs were all he deserved, he told me this story:

> When I was about twelve, our chimney developed
> a leak and it so happened that my room shared a
> wall with the chimney. The repairmen had to pull
> some boards off my wall in order to get at the chim-
> ney. After they fixed it, they left the boards leaning
> against another wall in my room, because my father
> told me that we would get insurance money from a
> claim on the repair job and that he would use that
> money to fix my wall. I went for about a month
> looking at a chimney through the bare studs in my
> room. When the money finally came in, my father,
> without telling me what he was doing, hired a con-
> tractor to improve *his* bedroom. He added a closet
> and fixed up his bathroom. After about another
> month I nailed up the old boards myself. I was sick
> of looking at the chimney. I was also sick of my
> father's selfishness. About a week after I nailed up
> the boards, I ran away from home.

What would it be like to look at a cold, bare chimney
while your father used money he promised you as a means
of getting what he wanted for himself? I asked Dan what
the message was in his father's actions. He said, "That I
was not worth the trouble even to put the old boards back
up, much less have the money to improve my room. It told
me that my needs were trivial, that *I* was trivial."

Unfortunately, Dan bought this message. When he
ran away from home, he was essentially looking for someone to nail up a few boards over a bare chimney. That is,
he was looking for some semblance of unselfishness in a
world that had, for him, become bare and cold. When the

two homosexuals offered to let him stay in the other side of their duplex, Dan was so desperate that he interpreted their crumbs as a form of acceptance. This acceptance would drip into his "approval tank" from time to time, and he interpreted these as periods of relative well-being. Most of the time, however, his "approval tank" would stay dangerously low, often lowering the door to the "shame tank." At these times of deep rejection and shame, Dan would be susceptible to drug abuse and one-night stands with promiscuous homosexuals.

Dan's lack of freedom is obvious. Everything he does is out of the necessity of avoiding a shame-attack. When shame does occur, his motivation becomes even more enslaved to necessity. In the midst of shame, Dan didn't even feel free to refuse anonymous sex combined with insane amounts of cocaine. Compulsion reigned supreme and freedom was nonexistent.

Dan's "food and drink" consisted of getting the approval of the two homosexual men next door. Knowing he couldn't guarantee their approval, he lived in quiet desperation. When they invited him into their circle, he munched hungrily on the crumbs they allowed him. When they excluded him, his emptiness goaded him into even more desperate measures. In either case, he knew no freedom of any kind.

Once Dan realized that Christ was willing to cleanse him and that he was designed for substantial "steak" in relationships, not crumbs, he was elated. His thankfulness grew as he saw the magnitude of what was wrong with him (sin) and the glory of what God had designed him for (unconditional love, deep impact). He stopped accepting crumbs from the two homosexuals. He moved out of the duplex.

It was a joyous day when Dan told me the story of a great victory. Having lost immediate control of Dan, his two previous consorts gave his name and number to a homosexual man "out looking for a good time." When this man called and proposed that he and Dan meet somewhere, Dan was able to refuse and to tell him that, because of Christ, he wanted no further part of that lifestyle. Dan's smile was wide because his freedom had become wide. No longer desperate for crumbs and having gained strength to look for "steak" in his relationship with God, Dan answered that phone call as a man growing in his freedom.

The leper, realizing what Christ has done, comes to the Deliverer and gives thanks. This realization and this thanksgiving lead to great freedom. No wonder: "It was for freedom that Christ set us free" (Galatians 5:1). The thankful man or woman begins to be delivered from the bondage of necessity, from the enslavement of compulsive living.

CHAPTER THIRTEEN

Moving Away from an Overactive Conscience by Cultivating Freedom

*Act as free men, and do not use your freedom as a
covering for evil, but use it as bondslaves of God.*
(1 Peter 2:16)

*For you were called to freedom, brethren; only do not
turn your freedom into an opportunity for the flesh,
but through love serve one another. For the whole
Law is fulfilled in one word, in the statement, "You
shall love your neighbor as yourself."*
(Galatians 5:13-14)

ONE REASON I CHOSE the first quote above was the fact
that Peter had so much trouble with the idea of freedom.
You might remember that God had to prod Peter with
a thrice-repeated vision before he was able to find the
freedom to obey God and preach to the Gentile, Cornelius
(Acts 10:9-48). Later, however, Peter reneged on this freedom. During a stay at Antioch (having arrived while Paul
and Barnabas were in the midst of evangelizing the Gen-
tiles there), Peter initially felt the freedom to eat with
the Gentile converts. But when a strict party of legalists arrived ("certain men from James"—Galatians 2:12),

Peter "began to withdraw and hold himself aloof, fearing the party of the circumcision" (2:12). Peter was afraid of the legalists and abandoned his own freedom.

The issue of Christian freedom hanging in the balance, Paul became so impassioned that he "opposed [Peter] to his face, because he stood condemned" (2:11). Paul felt so strongly about the freedom inherent in the gospel that he scolded a fellow apostle in public. Peter must have gotten the point, for he later says earnestly, "Act as free men." In other words, "Don't do what I did in Antioch; don't sell out your freedom for fear of disapproval."

GRATEFULNESS VERSUS DUTY AS THE MOTIVATION FOR OBEDIENCE

Peter is an example of a legalist journeying toward freedom. Before encountering the gospel, his whole life had revolved around a maze of rules and regulations, some of them biblical, some of them not. Along with the rest of the Jews, he had developed the dangerous assumption that God kept tabs on the number of religious rules he observed and was pleased according to the sheer regularity with which the rules were obeyed. Like the rest of the Jews, Peter had to be reminded, "I desire compassion, and not sacrifice" (Matthew 9:13). He had to see that God was a God of passionate love, not of wooden obedience. And, while love leads to obedience, it is an obedience that springs from the fire of gratefulness, not from the mechanics of duty.

Peter stumbled several times in his journey out of mere rule-keeping. It took repeated visions from God and, later, a strong, public scolding by Paul to bring Peter completely to his senses regarding the gospel. Paul saw that Peter failed because of his not being "straightforward about the truth of the gospel" (Galatians 2:14). What does it mean to be "straightforward" about the truth of the gospel? It means to refuse to deviate from the stunning freedom inherent in it. The heart of the gospel is that faith alone in the work of Christ is the source of salvation, and obedience to God (or disobedience) can do nothing to add (or detract) from the standing each of us has with God through Christ.

The implications of the gospel are enormous, but in a book about false guilt, I must single out one in particular. *The gospel implies that if we are dependent on the favor of others, we are violating the work of Christ.* Paul, as he sought to correct the Galatians about being led astray from the gospel, asserted that speaking in favor of the gospel will not please some: "For am I now seeking the favor of men, or of God? Or am I striving to please men? If I were still trying to please men, I would not be a bond-servant of Christ" (Galatians 1:10).

The point is clear: Fallen man is not naturally attracted to the gospel. This is true whether the gospel is verbalized or simply lived out. Fallenness always opposes the gospel. To the extent that a believer is controlled by his fallenness, to that extent will even a believer recoil from the implications of the gospel. Obviously, the Galatians are a case in point. Paul was writing to Christians in a large region of Asia Minor to correct their growing distaste for the gospel's implications for life. One of Paul's major points was that the gospel transforms *all* of the believer's new life, not just its beginning. He says, "Are you so foolish? Having begun by the Spirit, are you now being perfected by the flesh?" (Galatians 3:3). The Christian life is begun by a work of the Holy Spirit. Christ Himself said, "The wind blows where it wishes and you hear the sound of it, but do not know where it comes from and where it is going; so is everyone who is born of the Spirit" (John 3:8). The sovereign Spirit governs the beginning of a new life in Christ, and He is to govern all aspects of the progress of that life. Dependence on any other source of fuel for motivation is so foolish

that Paul likens it to being "bewitched" (Galatians 3:1).
Pursuing another source of life, says Paul, is so deviant
that doing so is like being under an evil spell.

DO WE REALLY BELIEVE
THAT IT IS WELL WITH OUR SOUL?

Living out the gospel, then, is antithetical to a lifestyle that
is bound up with milking others for favor and approval.
Such a wrong dependence is used as an alternative source
of life. To so depend on others is to say, "It is not well with
my soul." The gospel shouts just the opposite. It is so well
with our soul, that if we take the gospel seriously, we have
to conclude that all such attempts to protect and nourish
our inner being are silly. They are silly because our inner
man is secure in the keeping of Christ. We can't add to the
soul's security. We can only add to our *illusion* that our
soul is somehow more secure when we get approval from
others.

Once we get over this illusion, this insanity that we
can improve on what God has done, we are both delighted
and stunned to see that the task of finding our ultimate
well-being is over. "It is finished," said Christ. He meant
that His atoning work was complete, and He also implied
that all who embrace it are through with providing for
their own inner well-being.

HARM VERSUS DAMAGE

The gospel is so abrupt as to be disruptive. It deposits a
shocking reality: *All forms of insecurity are false.* Why?
Because it is well with our soul. Insecurity stems from
the feeling of being endangered, the feeling that things
are not well. But how can a life that is "hidden with Christ
in God" (Colossians 3:3) be endangered in any meaningful
way? Obviously, *harm* can be done to us—our feelings may

be profoundly hurt, relationships may be severely painful, the body may be traumatized, the organs may become diseased or aged—but can real *damage* be done to the "self" that will live eternally?

If we are "in Christ" (the New Testament's favorite phrase for describing a Christian), we are safe, not from harm but from real damage. Jesus alludes to our security when He says, "Do not fear those who kill the body, but are unable to kill the soul; but rather fear Him who is able to destroy both soul and body in hell" (Matthew 10:28). Two potential sources of insecurity are identified here: (1) all those who can hurt or destroy the body (in this context, He is referring to persecution that will come to His disciples from the Jewish religious leaders, but in principle His words cover all nondivine sources of harm) and (2) God Himself, who is able to act as Destroyer, not only of the body but the soul as well.

Jesus does not say that the first group will be entirely neutralized this side of Heaven. In fact, His earlier words, "A disciple is not above his teacher" (10:24), imply that His disciples should expect persecution. Harm will be done; persecution will follow the believer. Jesus never promises that His followers will be removed from harmful events in this world. He does, however, affirm that His people will be secure from ultimate damage. How do we know this? *The only One who has the power to damage the soul has promised never to exercise that power toward the believer.* In fact, after describing God as the ultimate Destroyer, Jesus goes on to say, "Are not two sparrows sold for a cent? And yet not one of them will fall to the ground apart from your Father. But the very hairs of your head are all numbered. Therefore do not fear; you are of more value than many sparrows" (10:29-31).

Far from being destroyed by the Destroyer-God, the believer is highly valued by a Father who is intimately and protectively involved with him. Again, the gospel cuts across our anxieties by telling us in no-nonsense tones that all our insecurities are false.

A Painful Journey Out of Cowardice

How hard is it to get this through our anxious head? We often find that we are incredibly stubborn at rejecting the security and freedom God offers. We have to pry open, one finger at a time, our frantic grip on our insecurities. Our courage grows painfully and slowly. Much of the time, we are still cowards.

Why are we so committed to an anxious view of life? Why are we willing to hole up in the confining fortress of our insecurities? Why do we reinforce the fortress with the thick walls of an overactive conscience, walls held together by the mortar of impeccable performance? Simply put, we hide in our fortress because if we venture outside it, we may be overwhelmed. Ultimate, irreversible damage might catch us in the open and swallow us up.

For me personally, the damage would most likely come in the form of being shamed and humiliated unexpectedly. The point, though, is that we all suffer from a fear of ultimate damage. We tend to see ourselves as endangered people whose only hope is to be resourceful enough to protect ourselves.

The Enslaving Fear of Death

The writer of Hebrews touches on our common dread by revealing that Jesus took on human flesh so that "through death He might render powerless him who had the power of death, that is, the devil; and might deliver those who through fear of death were subject to slavery all their lives" (Hebrews 2:14-15). Here we are confronted with an astonishing clarity: *No one who fears death can taste freedom.* Those who fear death are "subject to slavery all their lives." A corollary of this is that those who are subject to slavery (those who are enslaved to protecting themselves, for example) are being driven by a fear of death.

This fear runs deep, and it makes it easy for us to compromise our freedoms in Christ. Peter quickly departed from his freedom when a party of strict Jewish believers came from Jerusalem. Why? He was afraid of their censure. What did their disapproval carry that felt potentially so harmful to him? To ask it another way, why did Peter feel some of the same dread that had led him to deny Christ in the high priest's courtyard? Why would Peter deny the implications of the gospel just as he had denied Christ years before? Why would he return to legalistic enslavement when he was perfectly free to roam in the liberty of a Christian?

Both denials were based in Peter's insecurity. All his life, Peter had covered this insecurity with the bluff of self-sufficiency. His impetuous nature is well-known. What might be less well-considered is the idea that Peter's slapdash temperament may have been driven by a well-developed radar for meeting expectations. By living up to expectations in a bold, striking way, Peter hoped to find a place to belong. He made promises he couldn't keep ("Lord, with You I am ready to go both to prison and to death"—Luke 22:33), blundered into actions he couldn't sustain (walking on water), and offered his allegiance to whomever held the most power ("when they came, he began to withdraw and hold himself aloof, fearing the party of the circumcision"—Galatians 2:12). Ultimately, Peter was driven by the same fear of death the writer of Hebrews describes. Peter feared the death of his dream to belong somewhere, so much so that he often sold his allegiance to the highest bidder.

This dark thread in Peter's life highlights two crucial issues: (1) We can and must resolve our fear of death in order to experience freedom; (2) death takes many forms—both literal and figurative—so that our fear of death may take some very subtle shapes.

Moving Out of a Fear of Death

Let's first tackle this issue of resolving our fear of death and its resulting enslavement. The main principle is that *we must decide whether we will be motivated by fear of death or by the gospel's offer of life and ultimate security.* In order to develop this idea, I invite you to chew on an intriguing morsel from the novelist Walker Percy. With tongue in cheek, he divided humanity into two categories: the non-suicides and the ex-suicides.

The non-suicides are those who are still dominated by their fear of death. In their dread they would rather opt for some dysfunction, like depression, or for a numb, meaningless life than face the possibility of not existing. The non-suicides are in great pain, but they refuse to face that pain, preferring to anesthetize it through, say, depression. The ex-suicides, on the other hand, are those who have seriously entertained the idea of not existing any longer. They have faced the fact that perhaps their depression (or other pathology) is not pathological but simply logical.

Percy put it this way:

> You are depressed because you have every reason
> to be depressed. No member of the other two million
> species which inhabit the earth . . . would fail to be
> depressed if it lived the life you lead. You live in a
> deranged age—more deranged than usual, because
> despite great scientific and technological advances,
> man has not the faintest idea of who he is or what
> he is doing.[1]

In light of this desperate situation, Percy says it might be helpful to face the option of not existing at all, saying on the way out, "I do not care for life in this deranged world, it is not an honorable way to live; therefore, like Cato, I take my leave."[2] Once the option *not to be* is contemplated, it quickly emerges how empty it is. If we do choose to exit, everyone will soon be back doing the things they always did, and the world will continue to be a deranged place. Our exit wouldn't help anything at all. The most we would have done is take a shortcut out of our dread without working through it. Choosing *not to be* turns out to be the ultimate cop-out.

Now that we have seriously considered nonbeing, we can more carefully look at the choice *to be*. Once we admit that some form of pathology is one logical response to the crazed world we live in and once we have gone further to consider the emptiness of exiting altogether, we begin to envision a more alive way of being alive. That is, we begin to see that, even in a deranged world, we are *free*. If we don't have to fight off death any longer, perhaps it is also true that we don't have to fight off life. Perhaps it is true that life does not have to be based on slavery to fear. Or, as Percy says it:

> And you, an ex-suicide. . . . In what way have you
> been freed by the serious entertainment of your
> hypothetical suicide? Are you not free for the first
> time in your life to consider the folly of man, the
> most absurd of all the species, and to contemplate
> the comic mystery of your own existence? And even
> to consider which is the more absurd state of affairs,
> the manifest absurdity of your predicament: lost in
> the Cosmos and no news of how you got into such
> a fix or how to get out—or the even more preposter-
> ous eventuality that news did come from the God of
> the Cosmos, who took pity on your ridiculous plight
> and entered the space and time of your insignificant
> planet to tell you something. . . .
>
> The difference between a non-suicide and an ex-
> suicide leaving the house for work, at eight o'clock
> on an ordinary morning:
>
> The non-suicide is a little traveling suck of

care, sucking care with him from the past and being sucked toward care in the future. His breath is high in his chest.

The ex-suicide opens his front door, sits down on the steps, and laughs. Since he has the option of being dead, he has nothing to lose by being alive. It is good to be alive. He goes to work because he doesn't have to.[3]

Now, why would a Christian even think in this direction? Isn't it a bit silly for a believer in Jesus Christ to stop and look at the option of not existing? Why should we waste our time even opening up this category of nonbeing? The answer is that most western-culture Christians in the twentieth century *already* live as if nonbeing is the best option. That is, many believers are numb, hollow, stunted, and fearful. They are either the conformist dead or the conformist obnoxious. Both are unattractive. Neither carry any credibility for the cause of Christ. Most nonChristians look at the non-aliveness of Christians, yawn, and write them off.

How can we for whom Jesus paid with His life have so little life about us? It is because, as the writer of Hebrews says, we are enslaved all our lives to the fear of death. How do we get past this? How do we become "ex-suicides," those who shake off their fixation on death? My response is that we must face the death we are afraid of.

The Subtle Forms of Death that Dominate Us

This brings up the second issue embedded in that dark thread of Peter's life: the need to recognize that death takes many subtle forms. *We are not afraid only of death but of anything that reminds us of it.* The following paragraph gives a clear example of how fear of death can be transferred to other events and people that only represent the coming of death:

Another source of Joyce's tears was her feeling that she and Jack [from whom she was divorcing] had shared many lovely and important experiences. Without their union, these events, she felt, would perish. The fading of the past is a vivid reminder of the relentless rush of time. As the past disappears, so does the coil of the future shorten. Joyce's husband helped her to freeze time—the future as well as the past. Though she was not conscious of it, it was clear that Joyce was frightened of using up the future. She had a habit, for example, of never quite completing a task: if she were doing housework, she always left one corner of the house uncleaned. She dreaded being "finished." She never started a book without another one on her night table awaiting its turn.[4]

I find it hard to ignore Joyce's experience. In my own life, I have noticed occasional feelings of uneasiness when I can't remember the details of a special time, say, a vacation. I find myself, at times, wanting to capture it perfectly in memory, and when I can't, I become uncomfortable. There is a sense that something is being lost and it is absolutely crucial to retrieve it. When it can't be retrieved, something squirms anxiously inside. Why would it be so important for the past to be preserved? Because the more I can hang on to the past, the more I can slow down the devouring future. Why does the future feel "devouring"? Because the future is the signal that death is coming.

But aren't Christians supposed to be free from death-anxiety? Aren't believers those who have made their peace with death because Christ has taken the sting out of it? Didn't Jesus conquer death once and for all? Yes, yes, and yes; but we've already seen that what Christians profess often competes with a deeper set of largely unexamined convictions that influence much of their behavior.

Is it possible, then, that many of us hold vague but powerful ideas about death that enslave us? To say "no" to this question would seem to contradict the words of Scripture we have been considering: "that through death He might render powerless him who had the power of death, that is, the devil; and might deliver those who through fear of death were subject to slavery all their lives" (Hebrews 2:14-15). Clearly, fear of death is a major issue. On the basis of this passage alone, a biblical view of man would have to take humanity's fear of death seriously. Further, it would have to give space to the fact that the devil ("him who had the power of death") uses the fear of death to manipulate human beings into paralysis. And, in view of the paralysis of most Christians, it would seem fair to wonder how much of our numbness stems from the fact that Satan has been successful in his manipulating even believers into a fear of death.

What are some ways that Christians might evidence their fear of death? Death has many relatives that bring great fear. One of the closest relatives is the letting go of anything that we feel has contributed to our survival in a hard, sometimes lonely world. Giving up the things we have counted on for life feels like death to us, and we deeply fear the letting go. When we are asked to relinquish things that have kept us alive, our reluctance to let them go stems from an intense fear of what feels like death to us.

The things that have kept us safe and alive in a hard world have driven us toward self-sufficiency. We depend, not on God, but on our own strategies for making life feel bearable. Our strategies make us independent of God. This is why we need to let go of them. Yet, as I've said, letting go feels like death.

Because fear of death brings enslavement (as Hebrews 2:15 says), we end up not only being self-sufficient but also being *enslaved* to self-sufficiency. *Our strategies for self-sufficiency must be put to death before we can enter the freedom Christ came to give us.*

The guilt-driven conscience generates a particular set of strategies for self-sufficiency. All of them limit our freedom. False guilt is a major enemy of our Christian freedom. All of the strategies of an overactive conscience must die if we are to gain our freedom. Yet we deeply fear allowing them to die. They feel so crucial to our survival that we desperately fear their death. Here are some of the deaths that we fear.

The death of a negative self-image. Let's expand here on what was said earlier about a low self-image. The idea that a person with an overactive conscience would actually fear the death of a negative self-image might seem odd at first. Anyone would be happy to get rid of a low self-image, right? Not so fast. If this were true, it would be easy enough to change a negative self-image through logic alone. The difficulty of doing this is captured in the ensuing dialogue:

> COUNSELEE: I just don't feel like I have anything to offer.
>
> COUNSELOR: That's nonsense! You're bright, witty, thoughtful, popular. People enjoy being with you. You get invited to all kinds of social events.
>
> COUNSELEE: Yeah, but that's because I put up this big front—all smiles and on top of things. Inside, I'm so down on myself, I'd be mortified if anyone found out.
>
> COUNSELOR: How could you be down on yourself? People don't just like you for the externals. Everyone knows you have a big heart. One of the things they admire most about you is your volunteer work with the homeless.
>
> COUNSELEE: There's nothing to that. Anyone could do it.

COUNSELOR: But most people don't. There must be something special about you to keep that commitment.
COUNSELEE: Well, it's kind of you to say that.

In the last sentence, the counselee has just written off the counselor. Her words are a polite way of saying, "You are not talking anywhere near where I really live, so let's just agree to drop this subject." The counselor has no idea that this counselee works with the homeless because she sees herself in them: lonely, discarded, and unattractive. She doesn't love the homeless so much as she identifies with them. His use of logic to change her self-image only makes her feel more hopeless to communicate where she really struggles. His logical counterpoints to her negative self-statements have no impact on the way she actually feels about herself. In the end, she ends up taking care of him by letting him think his compliment has sunk in.

What she really needs to hear is something like this:

COUNSELEE: I don't feel like I have anything to offer.
COUNSELOR: You would be afraid to live without that feeling.
COUNSELEE: What do you mean?
COUNSELOR: You thrive on the feeling of not have anything to offer.
COUNSELEE: That's ridiculous. It's a miserable way to live.
COUNSELOR: No doubt it is, on one level. But on another level, it works quite well to live under the commitment that you have nothing to offer.
COUNSELEE: What do you mean, it works? It doesn't work well at all. Like I said, it's miserable believing I have nothing to offer anyone.
COUNSELOR: Let me show you how it works: You haven't offered me anything of yourself since

we've been meeting.

COUNSELEE: Like what?

COUNSELOR: You've never allowed yourself to cry in my presence when you're sad.

COUNSELEE: Oh, I couldn't do that.

COUNSELOR: Why not?

COUNSELEE: That's too personal.

COUNSELOR: What do you mean by "personal"?

COUNSELEE: You know, private.

COUNSELOR: Like I wouldn't know where your tears and feelings were coming from?

COUNSELEE: Yeah. And you might think they're weird.

COUNSELOR: So, by believing they're not worth offering to me, you end up preventing rejection.

COUNSELEE: Yes.

COUNSELOR: That's what I mean. You are happy to believe that you don't have anything to offer, because offering yourself might bring rejection.

This person battled with putting her low self-image to death. It worked well for her, by doing two things: (1) It shrank her world, and (2) it made it predictable.

How does a low self-image shrink one's world? Notice what happens in the dialogue. The counselee's feeling that she has nothing to offer rules out the option of crying in front of the counselor. She has effectively shrunk her world. She has reduced her freedom by carefully cultivating (with the help of important relational disappointments along the way) the fiction that she has nothing to offer. *She lives in a small world where the offer of tears is seen as embarrassing.* Her own humanity is stifled. This is the goal of a low self-image, to smother any alive humanness that might not be accepted by others.

Notice, too, that her poor view of herself makes her world more predictable. Faced with the fork in the road of showing her emotions or not, she has already predicted what she will do. It is inconceivable to cry when you believe beforehand that you have nothing to offer, including the tears of your own humanness.

The person with a guilt-driven conscience lives in a world that is small and calculated. This world feels safe, because the script is already written. And it will stay written as long as it is fueled by a low self-image.

The death of living by performance-based approval. The overactive conscience dictates that the only ticket to acceptance is to perform impeccably. Under this tyranny, the individual wakes up every morning under a pile of debits and with zero credits. He labors all day long to pile up credits and cancel the debits by performing to exhaustingly high standards. When the day is through, if there have been no setbacks during the day, he is just able to feel that his credits slightly outweigh his debits. But when he wakes up the next morning, he has to start over. Somehow, during the night, all his credits got transferred to the debit column!

What is even more amazing is that the individual himself made the transfer! He refuses each morning to recognize his credits because he fears to live without the spur of performance. How can he get approval without flawless performance? What other coin does he have with which to buy acceptance? Thus, instead of relaxing into his credits, he shoulders the pile of debits again and goes off wearily to meet the day. The debits act as a whip, lashing him into the level of performance he needs to feel that he has any credits. It would actually feel like death for him to assume that acceptance is based on grace instead of works. Believing that he must accumulate lots of "good works" before he will be accepted, he culti-vates the assumption that he has many faults (debits). His "good works" revolve around successfully compensating for those faults.

One of my counselees, Bobbie, told the story of her father's rejection of her mother and his inviting her to be his surrogate wife. Although no incest took place, her father illicitly wrapped his arms around her on an emotional level as a substitute for the wife he considered disdainful. He took Bobbie on business trips with him. They would do things together that should have been construed as his dating her. Instead of pursuing his God-given, hard-to-love wife, this man took the easy road of inviting his vulnerable daughter into a relational role that she was not built to bear.

But she thought that, to keep her parents' marriage together, she had to acquiesce to her father's pursuit of her. She believed that it was her duty to prevent the dissolution of her family. Even though she was in over her head, she thought herself duty-bound to keep slogging forward in being her father's "wife" emotionally. She thought, too, that it was her fault that the family wasn't perfect; and the only way she could correct her fault was to rescue the family by being the surrogate spouse her father wanted.

This began a pattern of searching for approval by the performing of misguided duty. Later, in her own marriage, when her husband signaled that he would bury himself in his work, she assumed that it was her job as a "submissive wife" to take on the parenting role single-handedly. Performing this misguided duty was, she thought, the only route to gaining approval. She could successfully compensate for her "faults" by being a strong pillar for her family.

Unfortunately, this led to an unhealthy equilibrium in which her husband was allowed to be passive. His passivity infused the marriage with a deadness that had a strong impact on their children, both of whom developed deep distortions in their own lives. Bobbie's duty-bound, all-consuming performance left little room for her family to express anything but their own unhealthiness in protest against her seeming omnipotence.

Dying to this pattern of performance-based approval was agonizing for Bobbie. Everything inside her screamed that recognizing her limits and requiring her husband to shoulder the leadership of the family would make her unbearably vulnerable. She would be vulnerable to rejection ("How can you be worth having around if you don't take care of everyone in your life?") and to the idea of trusting her husband's new initiatives.

On the other hand, she wanted deeply to believe that it was okay for her not to be in over her head all the time. She thirsted for a life where she could admit her limits and relax into the caring arms of someone else. Her fear of death (in the form of vulnerability) competed strongly with her thirst for life and freedom. Eventually, after many crises and setbacks, she embraced the gospel's implications: Life and security are in Christ, not in impeccable, wearisome performance.

The death of relationships as avenues of exchange. The overactive conscience endorses seduction as a lifestyle. The seduction is not sexual but emotional. That is, the guilt-driven conscience drives a person to look incessantly for ways to induce others to hand over approval, affirmation, and acceptance. The primary tactic is to offer oneself to others in the role of harmless helper. With false guilt in mind the person promises never to cut across your agenda and to be of help to you as you carry out that agenda. His hope is that you will enjoy him as an asset and "pay" him in that coin of approval he so desperately needs.

Years ago, I had a secretary whose guilt-driven conscience on one level made her an employer's dream. She was so dutiful that she would cover for me on phone calls I wanted to avoid, telling the caller I wasn't available, even when I was not particularly busy. There was one caller who was especially persistent and unpleasant, expressing her own emotional problems by calling obsessively. I really needed to deal with that caller honestly and help her see the distortions in her behavior. Instead, I relied on my dutiful secretary to screen those calls. I saw her as an asset in helping me avoid an unpleasantry. In reality, I was using her to avoid my responsibility to love this obsessive caller as Christ would. Yet my secretary never felt used because her own "twistedness" included false guilt and she lived for the approval I gave her when she helped me avoid a messy situation.

Our relationship had nothing to do with living out the gospel as two redeemed people (both of us are believers). Rather, we entered into an agreement that our relationship would be a medium of exchange. She would help me avoid the unpleasant; I would supply her the approval she craved. Every day, we courteously used each other as emotional vending machines. The courtesy was there to cover up this nauseating dance of mutual manipulation.

The overactive conscience makes human beings into interchangeable parts in a framework of buying and selling. Others simply become vendors of approval and affirmation with whom we barter, offering them the coin of dutiful, impeccable performance.

One counselee told me the story of having a brief affair some twenty years before while on a business trip. Years later, he decided to be honest with his wife about it. She was able to work through it to some degree and offer him a measure of forgiveness. Yet, years after he chose to be honest, she still struggled with the fact that he had given himself to another woman. He began to be impatient with her lack of forgiveness.

When he expressed this in a counseling session, I said words to this effect, "Your affair reminds your wife that all you want is someone who is turned on sexually by you. The first time another woman indicated that you turned her on, you had an affair with her. This tells your wife that you don't want *her*; you simply want someone who is excited by you sexually. That means that your wife could be *anyone* who is sexually aroused by you. Your wife lives every day with the reality that she is a faceless nobody whose only job is to show sexual arousal and thus validate your ego." His wife agreed and went on to express that she felt like a prostitute. Her only truly desired feature was her capacity to be sexually aroused by her husband. She experienced herself as anonymous, having no real identity.

While the husband certainly didn't have his affair out of an overactive conscience, this illustrates on a sexual level that, when a guilt-driven conscience becomes a factor in one or both parties of a relationship, this same anonymity occurs. My secretary, for example, could have been anyone so long as she was willing to help me avoid those unwanted calls. I wasn't loving her as Christ would but using her as an asset (and assets are interchangeable as long as they are identical in value). By the same token, she was using me to get the approval she needed.

Both of us needed to die to the commitment to use our relationship as an avenue of exchange. Years later, I had a secretary who understood that relationships are not to be giving-to-get arrangements. She noticed my pattern of avoiding difficult phone calls. One day, she confronted me about it. She was tactful but clear, and after some initial defensiveness, I had to admit that she was right and that I was being loved well. In her respect for me, she challenged me to become more the man whom God had designed.

Her relationship to me was not a medium of exchange. She got nothing out of taking the risk of exposing my pattern. I could have maintained my defensiveness and made it clear that she was the subordinate in the relationship. The risk was all hers. But she loved me enough to pierce my heart with a one-way arrow of strong compassion. Rather than exhibiting the slavery that false guilt generates ("I'll keep screening these calls even though he really should take them"), she showed great freedom in choosing to confront me. Because she walked in freedom, my weakness was exposed and I was given a clear opportunity to embrace a deeper maturity. Because she did not walk in fear of death, I was challenged to embrace life on new levels.

Death of a commitment to be the "good guy." The overactive conscience dictates that, in every situation, each of us must emerge as the "good guy." Since the overactive conscience's agenda is to foster the intake of approval from others, it refuses to jeopardize the soul's supply of well-being by contradicting the image it has so carefully cultivated. The image of being the good guy is pivotal for maintaining the inflow of approval from others. Our false guilt, then, dictates that our agenda in most settings is to keep the "good guy" persona intact. We watch carefully for the expectations of others and strive to satisfy them. Our seduction of others works! We offer compliance in exchange for approval. We become the "nice guy" in order to be seen and rewarded as the "good guy."

There are a number of tactics for guaranteeing a good guy image. One has been mentioned before, that of always being an asset and never a liability. The hidden agenda behind being this kind of asset dictates, ironically, that we can never be the kind of asset others truly need. By pulling for their approval we end up catering to others' unhealthy agendas by encouraging them to respond to a seduction. When I succeed in complying with them and being rewarded by them, I have corrupted the relationship. Seduction and corruption are not exactly relational bedrock. In fact, the relationship is only as strong as the latest level of compliance and reward. There is no commitment to the *persons* involved, only a commitment to the relationship as a vehicle of harvesting the crop of self-protection. That crop is only as abundant as our ability to be the "good guy" that others "need."

Another tactic for being the good guy is that of not

rocking the boat. The good guy seeks to help others carry out their agendas in hopes of a reward. One woman told of her frustration at having to meet an unreasonable dead-line each week. By Wednesday morning, she had to pro-duce a document that would be used the following Mon-day. This meant she had two days each week to gather materials, type, lay out, print, and copy the document. For years, she endured the pressure in frustrated, ulcerous silence.

Through a relationship with a good friend, she was confronted with her tendency not to rock the boat, even when the boat needed to be rocked. At length, she pres-ented her boss with her frustrations and proposed that the deadline be moved to Thursday. He resisted at first, then admitted that a Wednesday deadline had allowed him to procrastinate in his decisions as to how best to present the document each Monday. By rocking the boat, this secretary offered her boss a relationship built on "truth in love" rather than on "compliance for reward." The relationship went from being laced with seduction to being infused with sanctification.

A third tactic for ensuring a good guy image is that of monitoring and lowering tension in relationships. The person with an overactive conscience acts as a thermo-stat. When he feels relational tension, this person works hard to keep the tension to a minimum. If tension gets out of hand, his agenda of getting approval will be wrecked since irritated people do not give out approval.

I'll never forget an incident that made my guilt-driven conscience obvious to me and a roomful of people. It hap-pened when my wife and I were team-teaching a fifth-grade Sunday school class with another couple. Unknown to me, the other couple had decided to stage a mock argu-ment. Their intent was to use the staged quarrel as an object lesson for the Bible study that would follow. When they began to argue over whose fault it was that they had left the lesson manual at home, my "good guy" thermostat went berserk. While the fifth-graders calmly watched this argument, I jumped up and began searching through my briefcase for my lesson manual. If I could produce it quickly enough, maybe I could defuse the tension that felt so dangerous to me.

My fear of death (the death embedded in intense tension and its disruption of my subtle, "good guy" agenda) enslaved me to a knee-jerk reaction to this couple's quarrel. My lack of freedom in the face of anger was obvious. Anyone could control me through the expression of anger or tension. My compulsive commitment to be a "thermostat" severely limited my options. In the face of anger, the question "What would it mean to love this angry person?" never entered my mind.

A fourth tactic for being the good guy has already been touched on: that of always being "nice." I put *nice* in quotes, because it is *not* nice to seduce people. The kind of niceness that is aimed at self-protection is never appropriate. Niceness on this level is a denial of the gospel. It is a declaration that we need approval because it is not well with our soul.

Is it "nice" for a secretary to protect her employer from his moral obligation to love others as Christ would? Is it "nice" for me to model to fifth-graders an obsession with tension reduction? Of course not. This kind of "niceness" is simply seduction masquerading as kindness.

The truth is that such "niceness" is rooted in cowardice. While this may sound harsh, it is simply another way of describing the slavery that emerges from our fear of death. The writer of Hebrews says that Christ came to "render powerless him who had the power of death" (2:14). Jesus came to take from Satan the power to subject human beings "to slavery all their lives" through fear of death. The gospel says, then, that we need not cower before death (in any form) one moment longer.

How does this relate to niceness? Niceness reflects my conviction that death lurks in anger, tensions, or contempt from others. Our fear of death finds its expression in "niceness" that is designed to keep the sword of anger, etc., in its sheath. If we can keep others' "swords" put away, we can continue the seduction on which we so desperately depend for life. If others do "draw the sword," we must shift from seduction to fight or flight. Either way, our pipeline for approval is shut off. Our anxious soul, feeling dependent on the nourishment of approval, begins to starve. Our overactive conscience searches frantically for a way to reopen the approval pipeline.

One counselee, a man who had terribly violated his wife and children, tried mightily through several sessions to blame me for his wife's resistance to him. He insinuated over and over that if I would conduct the counseling differently, his wife would see her faults and embrace the relationship as before. My response was to continue to point out the clear data that he had fostered an abusive home. When he saw that I was immoveable, he switched the battleground to a financial one, insisting that he could not afford my fee (even though earlier, he knew how to resolve this). Since I have a long history as a "nice guy," this tactic played into my old internal "scriptures"—e.g., "never, ever look selfish, even if you have to compromise your principles to do so."

Having already done battle with this man over his violation of his family, it was tempting for me to capitulate in this new skirmish. I was deeply pulled to repeat earlier assurances that financial arrangements could be made. I felt a real possibility that this man would pull out of counseling, spraying anger on me as he went, shutting off my approval pipeline, and branding me a failure for "letting" his marriage stay at an impasse.

On the other hand, I knew that his agenda was not to face his own failure honestly but to redirect the sessions toward blaming his wife or me. His message was, "If my marriage doesn't work, it's your fault." As he argued his financial straits, I simply said, "You've made your point. Just call and let me know if you'll be here next week." The session was over.

I wanted him to leave with the ball in his court. But my overactive conscience screamed, "Are you crazy? It's not nice to stand your ground. You're not in control of your own safety! What if he pulls the sword of anger? Of shame? Of threatening harm to your reputation? You fool, you're in for it now! You'd better reconsider." Notice the tyranny of the overactive conscience. It threatens that without the tool of "niceness" all is lost. There will be danger, loss of control, loss of the "food" the soul must have to survive.

This is the tyranny that is the sworn enemy of Christian freedom. The overactive conscience is a dictator and a bully. It prods each of us to be "nice" by broadcasting very un-nice messages to our frightened soul. In essence, the guilt-driven conscience is us attacking ourselves with demands and threats in order to keep our world as safe as possible, subduing ourselves so that we don't "get carried away" into the terrifying dizziness of freedom. The result? A bland, inoffensive "nice guy," a success at staying safe, but a dismal failure at being a pungent aroma of life to the righteous and of death to the wicked.

WHAT KIND OF "GUY" SHOULD WE BE?

I want to use this insistence on emerging as the "good guy" to raise a momentous question: What kind of person does God want you and me to be? Before you answer that question too quickly ("God wants me to be as much like Christ as possible"), stop and reflect. What kind of person are you really? It is one thing to give the right answer (God expects Christlikeness), it is quite another to *live* the right answer.

While we know what God desires of us, we often live

in a way that contradicts what we know. Again, there can be a wide gap between what we profess and the real convictions under which we live. We can profess the goal of Christlikeness even as we churn out a "nice guy" persona triggered by the tyranny of false guilt.

How can we follow Christ as King when we cower under a tyrant? How can He be our Master when we cultivate an overactive conscience fueled by slavery to a fear of death? These questions should not promote discouragement but excitement. They open a door into freedom that is both frightening and exhilarating. Actually, the door is more like a hallway than an immediate entry. Making Christ truly our Lord is a process.

Starting this process, entering this hallway is a matter of asking the questions: "What kind of person does God want me to be?" *and* "What kind of person am I right now?" Answering this latter question requires enormous honesty and courage. I find that I must blast before I can build. I must see clearly what has to go before I can see I need to grow. I cannot enter freedom without first confronting and repenting of what enslaves me.

The target of our repentance must be our misdirected commitment to maintaining our overactive conscience. In the next chapter, I want to sketch a portrait of freedom. The person who emerges will be a composite of friends, relatives, and counselees, all of whom command my highest respect. They are men and women around whom evil is hard-pressed and righteousness is fanned into flame. The portrait's purpose will be to demonstrate the demanding but joyous journey toward freedom and its inviting impact as we move toward fruition.

CHAPTER FOURTEEN

A Portrait of Freedom

THE RADIO CAME ON at six in the morning. This woke John up. Sort of. His brain struggled, like an engine with a weak battery, to turn over. Finally, juiced up by a first coherent thought, his brain reluctantly began to idle. The thought, still blurred, was the same thought that had wakened him for some time now. It said, "There is something wrong with me."

He had forgotten, again, what to do with this. It was uncomfortable. It signaled for resolution. But he could not figure out where to put it at first.

He rolled over and looked groggily at his wife. Her mouth was open, and he peered toward it as if the answer might emerge. But the thought only got more uncomfortable. Somehow his wife figured in the pain of whatever was wrong with him.

He knew it wasn't physical. Nothing wrong there except a tendency to overeat. He began to feel as though he had crawled out of the cavern of sleep and into the cavern of pain. Nothing new there. He had exchanged one cavern for the other for years. Each morning he had simply rolled from the darkness of dull sleep into the darkness of dull pain.

Another thought began to juice up his brain. It turned over a bit faster. The thought was that there was something wrong with stopping at the fact that something was wrong with him. A light flickered at the end of the cavern of pain.

A tendency to overeat—that thought had gone by too fast. Something about food. Food and fear. Eating to feel better. Eating to bring a small candle into the cavern of pain. Food helped him feel good, gave him the feeling he was being cared for, a source of comfort in the cavern. Sitting in the cavern, eating his way into the small circle of light. Afraid of the dark beyond the circle, he dreaded when the candle would go out. Soon after he ate, it always faded. Sometimes, he had an extra dessert to keep it going. But, eventually, it always went out.

When the candle failed he would feel the weight of the dark. In it, he would "lie down in torment."

Wait. Where did that torment thing come from? More juice. The light at the end of the cavern strengthened slightly. Enough for him to realize it was not his own. Where did it come from? He wasn't yet sure, but he knew there was no torment in it.

No torment—that would be new. A lessening of torment. There was a vague delight in the thought.

His brain was almost humming. More light, less cavern. He was able now to go toward the light. It wasn't his own, he knew. Where was it from? Somebody. Not his wife. He felt a vague pain about her. But not the kind that pulled him back into the cavern. Somehow, it was a pain that propelled him toward the light.

A light from somebody. Not his wife, but relating to her. More light was coming. Something was wrong with him, but—don't stop there, don't ever stop there—light was there from somebody. And it had to do with what was wrong with him. The light came through his wife somehow, but not from her. When he looked at the light through his wife, he could see what was wrong with him.

He didn't like it. When he saw the light through his wife, it was impossibly bright. It was exposing. It was bright, bright, bright. He felt a pull to go back toward the darkness of the cavern. But the pull was not from the light. Even though the light wounded him, it drew him. The pull didn't wound, but it smothered. It hid torment within it.

Torment—now that was a thought full of juice. His brain came fully to life. The light bathed his brain like oil and made it go.

He relaxed a bit. No more cavern. Light like oil, a humming brain. Why not put it in gear? When he did, it took him directly to the woman beside him. He looked at her again. Her mouth was still open. He stopped to listen.

She spoke to him now. Every glimpse of her spoke distinctly to him. There was a time she had been mute. Well, actually, he had been deaf. He had been deaf on purpose. Afraid that hearing her would put out his occasional candle, he had hunched over his meals, a deaf man, and sucked light and comfort from a fork. Cold light. Brittle comfort. But it was all he had.

He put his ear close to her mouth. Her whispering breath was as loud as the light was bright. She told him what was wrong with him. He nodded. He remembered. He thanked her. He kissed her cheek. And another thought hit him: "There is someone else to kiss." He got up, put on slippers, and padded to the kitchen for coffee.

When his lips touched the hot liquid he thought again, *Someone else to kiss.* Somehow that wasn't quite all of it. Ah. Someone had kissed him as well. Someone had kissed him with a kiss of love. He sat down with his coffee. Someone who loved him had kissed him. The kiss had something to do with what was wrong with him. He began to cry.

He noticed that he had been crying more lately. Before, he had cried maybe once a year. It was usually when some movie had sneaked in on him and pressed down on his loneliness and fear. By the time the credits rolled by, though, he always had it under control. Now he was crying all over the place, right out in the open sometimes.

He had taken to following his tears, trying to find out where they came from. Usually they came from the same place: Someone had kissed him even when something was badly wrong with him.

What was so big about that? Wouldn't a mother kiss her child when he was sick? Yes, but here was the thing: The child wouldn't be spitting in the mother's face while she kissed him.

That was it. The One who had kissed him had also been sullied by him. *While we were yet sinners,* he thought. The clean kissed the unclean and was made unclean. This was so the unclean one could be washed.

His tears were the overflow of being washed clean. Yes, he had sullied his wife and by doing so had spit into the face of his Creator. And this Creator had responded, not with a thunderbolt, not with a tribunal, but with an embrace!

In that embrace he felt small. He felt the kind of small that relaxes into the strength of someone greater. But he also felt the kind of small that is mean and petty. He was being embraced by Someone better than he. And his smallness was exposed and highlighted. Someone was returning good for his evil. This Creator was loving His enemy. And this love was "heaping burning coals" on his head.

He felt hot shame but with it no lessening of the embrace. In the midst of seeing his ugliness, he saw no lessening of the love in his Creator's eyes. This staggered him. It was a love that did not overlook his sin but probed it, pushed it forward and highlighted it, not for the purpose of counting it as evidence against him but so it could be pardoned.

He didn't even remember wanting this embrace. Because he didn't think it was possible. Every other relationship in his life had been a struggle over who deserved blame. Everyone worked mightily to avoid blame and pin it on someone else. Don't admit wrongdoing. Don't confess a fault. Because if you do, someone will make you pay.

So why ask for an embrace when there's never been one? Especially from Someone you've already spit on? He had hardened his heart. He had crouched in his cavern.

But the "wind blows where it wishes." He hadn't wanted the embrace, couldn't claim the credit of having begged for it, had already hardened his heart against it. That was why he had looked for a cheap embrace elsewhere. That was why there were pain lines around his wife's eyes.

At first, the cheap embrace had only involved looking for approval. Desperate for someone to applaud him, he listened intently for the smallest smattering of hand clapping. One day, he heard it in that secretary's words, "I sure like that cologne you wear."

"Oh," he said, tingling all over. "You've noticed it?"

"Yes," she said, "for a long time."

A long time! She said she'd noticed it for a long time! The applause was getting louder and much more interesting. It wasn't long before the cheap embrace turned from words to meetings to kisses to bed.

The real embrace had found him when the cheap one had blown up in his face. Someone else's cologne had smelled better. His wife had found notes she hadn't written him. The real embrace not only found him but hit him like a bus in the midst of failure, disgrace, and harm done.

He had held on with new life and found himself being loved with a heat that melted both his heart and his dross. He had been forgiven much. This was why he cried so much lately. He also found himself ruminating more. His coffee was cold. Salty places on his face begged for a shower. It was time for work.

That night found him in a different mood. A day of collisions with others whose hearts were still hard left him soul-weary and sore. Hard-won freedoms had been exercised with little response from others. Here and there he had loved well only to be spurned. Once or twice, he had embraced only to be stabbed.

The cavern of pain seemed closer, more seductive. Was it really worth it to live out of that embrace? Had the One who softened his heart provided anything to heal its new wounds?

He wasn't sure. All he knew was that he was seeing his wife as part of a tag team to help him get the kids in bed. Not a good sign. Whenever he reduced his wife to a function, bad things happened.

Too bad. He was too spent to worry about it. Somehow, they got the kids into bed. But not all the way. His oldest child had some concerns that could not be delayed.

She found him in the kitchen. Groggy and sad about the hardness of his heart, he was not really present. She didn't let that stop her. Putting all her six-year-old charm into her tone, she said, "Dad, you forgot to give me a hug and a kiss goodnight."

Absently, he leaned over and kissed her and gave a perfunctory hug. It seemed enough for her, and she padded back to bed.

Five minutes later, she was at his elbow again. "Dad, I forgot to get a drink of water." Too tired even to address the now-apparent issue of manipulation, he went through the ritual of meeting her reqest. She was gone, but his anger seemed stronger.

She came out again. Smiling innocently, she said, "I have a sore throat. Can I have a throat lozenge?"

He pawed through a drawer, handed it to her. "Now, you stay in bed," he growled.

She was not deterred. A few minutes later, she was

tugging on his shirt. "Dad, I think I heard a noise."

He steered her back into her bedroom and went through another ritual of checking the window, looking into the closet. "There," he said, "there's nothing to be afraid of. Mommy and Daddy will protect you and so will Jesus." After another hug and kiss, he left the room. His kiss had been briefer and his anger still more insistent than before.

It seemed that he hadn't even sat down when she was in the kitchen again, saying in a singsong voice, "Daddy, could you adjust the fan; I'm hot."

This time he boiled over. Loudly and with real malice, he shouted and pointed, "Get back in that room, young lady, or I'll make you sorry you ever had a daddy!"

He heard himself say these words and, worse, he heard the murderous tone that carried them into her soul. He saw her face fall, crashing from happiness to shame.

Without looking up, she turned and walked back toward her room. He followed, angry at himself and angry that her foolishness had exposed his own.

Suddenly his daughter turned, fixed her eyes on him, and said, "Dad, when you talk to me that way, I feel so stupid inside."

He stood, transfixed by this simple unfurling of the harm he had done to her soul. How he wanted to slide off the point! Something inside demanded to shift the blame to her and make a quick getaway from the spotlight of her words. After all, she had been the manipulative one. She had pushed him to the limit with her childish demands.

But her wounds cried out to him. *Your brother's blood cries out to me from the ground*, he thought. Sure, she had been manipulative. Yes, that needed to be dealt with at some point. But the real issue was that her foolishness had exposed his own. She revealed the pitiful fountain he had been drinking from, that of demanding to be weak and coddled at the end of a day when his efforts at loving hadn't received the hero's welcome he thought they deserved.

The question was this: Would he act on the freedom at the heart of the gospel? Someone had kissed him. Would he swim upstream against his anger and accept the rebuke of a child? This was true freedom, to accept exposure, no matter what its source—or its cost.

He knelt and put his hands on her shoulders. "Sweetie, I'm so sorry. Daddy has really failed you. I was wrong to shout at you like that."

Not quite ready for a confession, she said, "Oh, Dad, you didn't do anything wrong."

"Yes, I did do something wrong. I was speaking to you out of a bad place in my heart. And I hope you'll forgive me."

She hugged him. "I do forgive you, Daddy."

Sometime later, he lay in bed thinking. He was aware of the weapons he could have used to put his daughter in her place. When she said that he made her feel stupid inside, he could have roared, "You think you feel stupid now, just wait 'til you've had the spanking you're going to get!"

But somehow a breathtaking wind had blown into his heart at that moment and had shown him the righteousness in what she had said. He shuddered at the damage he could have done and wept at the grace that showed him the way. The freedom to love her well had been granted by One who always loves well. No wonder he was crying more. In both grief and joy.

What if he had just reacted? Instead of moving toward freedom, he would have snuffed her out, smothered the candle of her righteous rebuke, put her in her own cavern of pain.

How joyous not to bury her talent! How joyous to walk in freedom and be a haven for righteousness. *A haven for righteousness.* He turned over. There she was again, his sleeping wife. Her mouth was open. He put his ear near it again, and again her steady breathing was laced with whispers. What was she saying? "How wonderful," he heard, "to smell the strong aroma of masculinity that is expended *for* someone instead of the cheap scent of cologne from a weak man begging for applause."

REFLECTIONS ON THE "PORTRAIT OF FREEDOM"

An important implication of this "portrait" is that Christian freedom blossoms with the cultivation of a thankful heart. Luke's record of an immoral woman's (probably a prostitute) response to Jesus implies this relationship between freedom and thankfulness:

> Now one of the Pharisees was requesting Him
> to dine with him. And He entered the Pharisee's
> house, and reclined at table. And behold, there was
> a woman in the city who was a sinner; and when
> she learned that He was reclining at table in the
> Pharisee's house, she brought an alabaster vial
> of perfume, and standing behind Him at His feet,
> weeping, she began to wet His feet with her tears,
> and kept wiping them with the hair of her head,
> and kissing His feet, and anointing them with the
> perfume. Now when the Pharisee who had invited
> Him saw this, he said to himself, "If this man were
> a prophet He would know who and what sort of per-
> son this woman is who is touching Him, that she is
> a sinner."
>
> And Jesus answered and said to him, "Simon, I
> have something to say to you." And he replied, "Say
> it, Teacher." "A certain moneylender had two debt-
> ors; one owed five hundred denarii, and the other
> fifty. When they were unable to repay, he graciously
> forgave them both. Which of them therefore will love

him more?" Simon answered and said, "I suppose the one whom he forgave more." And He said to him, "You have judged correctly."

And turning toward the woman, He said to Simon, "Do you see this woman? I entered your house; you gave Me no water for My feet, but she has wet My feet with her tears, and wiped them with her hair. You gave me no kiss; but she, since the time I came in, has not ceased to kiss My feet. You did not anoint My head with oil, but she anointed My feet with perfume. For this reason I say to you, her sins, which are many, have been forgiven, for she loved much; but he who is forgiven little, loves little." And He said to her, "Your sins have been forgiven." And those who were reclining at table with Him began to say to themselves, "Who is this man who even forgives sins?" And He said to the woman, "Your faith has saved you; go in peace." (Luke 7:36-50)

The word "to thank" never appears in this story (there is no such verb in Hebrew or Aramaic).[1] Yet when Jesus asks about the two forgiven debtors, "Which of them therefore will love him more?" He is portraying a love that is so interlaced with thanksgiving that the two are practically synonymous. We can also see love and thanksgiving intertwined in Psalm 116:1 – "I love the LORD, because He hears my voice and my supplications." The word *thanks* is never used in this psalm, yet it is clearly a psalm of thanksgiving. The gratitude is simply expressed through love.

Luke, then, shows us an immoral woman who has been changed by Jesus. Her gratitude is so strong that she falls in love with Him. Her loving actions become a "psalm" of thanksgiving, an act of worship. In her passionate worship, she displays a freedom that breaks the constraints of "what is appropriate." Uninvited and unwelcome at the Pharisee's table, she nonetheless makes up her mind to thank Jesus the moment she learns of His whereabouts. The miracle of newness inside her led her into a freedom to go where she would never have dared go before.

Here is a picture of great liberation. The prostitute knows nothing but that she is forgiven, and in her joy, she freely gives herself to Jesus despite the social awkwardness. The Pharisee, on the other hand, is the picture of the guilt-ridden conscience, scrupulous and caught up in the question, "Is this appropriate?" Yet he is lax and thoughtless in matters of compassion. He is so intent on a piece of moral trivia (a real prophet wouldn't let an immoral woman touch him) that he completely misses a miracle of compassion (Jesus as the Friend of sinners).

The Pharisee also misses the contrast between the prostitute and himself. She displays a miracle: a changed and thankful heart. He demonstrates the dullness of a hard one. She cannot contain herself; he is so well-contained and self-satisfied that he becomes a symbol for those who are blind to the enormity of their sin and their need for forgiveness.

Do you know the freedom of a thankful heart? Have you received something more healing than the Band-Aid of an overactive conscience? Have you received the surgery of forgiveness for sin? Do you feel that what is truly wrong with you has been fully addressed through Christ and thus that it is well with your soul?

Christ's atonement brings thankfulness that brings freedom. The great freedom envisioned in these pages is freedom from a nitpicking, over-acute, and self-protecting conscience. Such a conscience kills love. It is a tyrant under whose self-critical magnifying glass we can be neither a haven for righteousness nor a danger to evil. All we are left with is a frantic scurrying after the expectations of others. What irony! We are reduced to picking through the scraps of affirmation that others leave us when the very God of Heaven is thunderous and unceasing in His acceptance of us and His love for us!

False guilt is a thief. It robs us—with our own cooperation—of the rich banquet of God's love and compassion and substitutes the crumbs of approval we have wrung from others through our willingness to walk the treadmill of meeting their expectations.

THE OVERACTIVE CONSCIENCE: DEAD TO GOOD AND INVITING OF EVIL

The first reflection on the above "portrait," then, is that freedom springs from a thankful heart. The second is this: The overactive conscience is neither a haven for righteousness nor a danger to evil.

You might protest at this point: How can an overactive conscience *not* be a haven for righteousness? Even if it's a bit overscrupulous, isn't it still filtering out some bad behaviors? My response is that the overactive conscience is not merely a hyperactive sentry guarding the gates of one's morality. Ironically, as we have seen, the guilt-driven conscience is not concerned at all with morality *per se.* Morality is not its aim. Rather, it uses apparent morality as a vehicle for getting approval. False guilt results in a dry compliance instead of a morality rooted in the passionate pursuit of God's character no matter the consequences.

Compliance is not godliness. It doesn't have the deep roots in passion for God that enable us to endure the consequences of obedience. For example, a man who finds his marriage growing stale and decides to handle it out of mere compliance is headed for disaster. There is a limit to the times he can take himself by the scruff of the neck and respond to a wife he finds increasingly dull. Compliance alone will give him a stiff, formal arrangement with his wife that may survive on frosty politeness for a time.

But sooner or later, this man will either become completely numb, or—more likely—he will crack and become an enraged, entitled victim who, blaming his wife for his shattered dreams, abandons his family. This is why so many "Eagle Scouts" of the 1940s and '50s did an about-face in the 1970s, '80s, and '90s and divorced their wives. They left (and are leaving) bloodied relationships and broken souls behind them in unprecedented numbers.

No one would have predicted it unless he had first asked the question, "Can a personality built on mere compliance sustain a commitment in the face of the inevitable struggles of marriage?" The answer, of course, is no. Compliance is only a way of "doing good" in exchange for a supply of validation and approval. A compliant man or woman in a marriage where the approval has dried up is simply a time bomb. The explosions are still going on throughout our social landscape, and the fuses are lit by compliance.

The overactive conscience is not a haven for righteousness. It is not concerned with true morality. In fact, it is really not a conscience at all. It is simply a selfish, anxious grasping for emotional supplies. The guilt-obsessed conscience can be visualized as two hands. One hand reaches out, probes for the expectations of others, and meets them. Then the other hand extends, grasping for the validation and approval that is supposed to come as part of the mutual trade arrangement. When the validation or approval stops, eventually it will be time to move on to other arrangements. Obviously, there is no haven for righteousness in such a sad setup.

Further, the overactive conscience is not a danger to evil. Compliance does not actually have the courage to oppose evil. Picture a woman—let's call her Mary—whose husband, an insecure and angry man, is embroiled in a fierce competition with his oldest son over who is the strongest male in the family. Although this rivalry is not consciously discussed, it is subtly and angrily acted out almost every day.

The adolescent son, under strict orders to show up on time for an extended-family holiday gathering, stays too long at the mall, his way of saying, "Your authority means nothing to me." He shows up a half-hour late, walking in as everyone is eating. His father, stung by his son's defying him in full view of everyone, decides to go public with his own anger. He shouts, "I told you to be here on time! Look how you've embarrassed your mother in front of everybody. Go to your room and forget about having anything to eat." The boy, equally stung by his father's public scolding, injects his reply with poisoned insolence, "I ain't going nowhere, old man."

To make a long story short, this showdown escalates until the father ends up chasing his son through the house with a baseball bat in front of horrified guests. This is when the son is fourteen. This time, he is cowed and brought back into line. When he is eighteen, he beats up his father and leaves the house forever.

Back at the holiday gathering, Mary is frozen with fear, anger, and embarrassment as the two males she loves most scuffle down the hall. Finally, she forces a smile, thinking it her duty to rescue the anguished guests. Her misguided attempt to smooth things over revolves around these words, "They really do love each other. They're just angry about other things. My husband is really frustrated at his job right now. Maybe we all need a vacation." Fighting back tears, she makes an attempt at humor: "I think next year we'll take the vacation *before* we have this get-together." She is working hard to lay a veneer of normalcy over the gaping hole this turf war has left in her family. Her overactive conscience sternly dictates that a good wife will not question her husband's choices even when they are clearly wrong. She is absolutely no danger to the evil in her husband's insecure, blind heart. For four more years she sweeps this conflict under the rug until her son gains the physical strength to pound his father into the carpet.

While she was not responsible for changing these two men, she was responsible for exposing their warfare as evil. She was responsible for speaking the truth in love (Ephesians 4:15). But her overactive conscience insisted on a cover-up. She became compliant. Evil was allowed to thrive in her family until it exploded triumphantly and left a shattered home.

What might a truly free woman have done differently? To get at this, we must explore how she might have *been* someone different. Her freedom to take a different path could emerge only from a strong embracing of the idea that it is well with her soul because of the atonement of Christ. Her growing sense of internal wholeness would allow her to break the "atone or die" cycle that fed her compliance. As she developed a greater sense of pardon, her gratefulness would more and more replace duty as her source of motivation. Gratefulness motivates by asking the question, "Since I have been so loved, how can I show Christ's love to others? Since my well-being is so well provided, how can I provide for the well-being of others?" This is the spirit embedded in Christ's words, "A new commandment I give you, that you love one another, even as I have loved you" (John 13:34).

Her motivation no longer springs from the shallow duty of sweeping harsh realities under the rug in an attempt to "be a submissive wife." Now, submission will take the form of aligning herself with Christ and then aligning herself under her husband *as one who wants his true well-being*. In those twin alignments, she will move with the freedom of real love rather than being stuck in shallow compliance.

At the holiday gathering, Mary might have responded to the scuffle between her husband and son with words like these, "Folks, I'm sorry you're having to see this. I'm embarrassed and tempted to make light of this whole thing, but I don't really want to do that. I've been realizing for some time what's happening between my husband and my oldest son. I hope you'll pray for me as I try to shed some light on it, especially for my husband since he is responsible to lead this family."

I can hear someone saying, "That sounds fine, but it's just too much to expect. People don't think that way and certainly don't talk that way." But people don't think and talk that way because they are enslaved to the task of providing for their own well-being. Thus they don't have the *freedom* to engage in thinking about what's really happening in their souls and in their families.

On the other hand, a real grasp of the atoning work of Christ and the well-being that is the Christian's birthright leads to a deep wrestling with previously avoided realities. The Christian is the only human who can afford to see what is really true without distorting it. Mary is now willing to see without the distorting glasses of false guilt, which bend everything to fit the demands of compliance. Seeing clearly, she shudders at the evil that has been clawing for so long at her family's fiber.

At the same time, she revels in the freedom to confront that evil, to become dangerous to it because of her great love for her husband and children. She mourns over the lame love of her former days, seeing it now as a thinly disguised, selfish compliance. But, through confession and repentance, she feels a fresh wind of God's Spirit moving her toward being a "soft warrior," deeply feminine, yet relentless in her kind and firm exposure of evil.

That night, Mary approaches her husband about his handling of their son:

> MARY: I need to tell you some of my feelings about what happened today.

TOM: What do you mean by "what happened today"?

MARY: Don't be evasive. You know very well what happened today with our son. I want you to know what I saw.

TOM: You saw a disobedient son get what he deserved. He'll learn to respect me or one of us will have to go.

MARY: That's not what I saw. I saw a threatened, insecure father lose control of his anger and abuse his son with a baseball bat.

TOM: I never hit him with that bat!

MARY: The abuse was not in hitting or not hitting. The abuse was in how you handled the whole situation.

TOM: You expect me to let him get away with that kind of disrespect?

MARY: You keep making him the problem. We both know he has some problems. But I'm talking about you. You were abusive.

TOM: I don't have to take this. You're starting to sound as uppity as him!

MARY: I'm not saying this to be uppity. I'm saying this because I do respect you.

TOM: You call this respect? I call it disloyalty.

MARY: I respect you so much that I'm willing to ask you to handle your anger with maturity.

These are the words of a woman who knows that, despite the turbulence of a sinful world, it is well with her soul. Tom may come against her hopeful soul in a strong, repulsive way; but he cannot ultimately damage her. She is operating out of the resulting freedom and is seeking to love him well. In so doing, she has become both a haven for righteousness and a danger to evil.

Someday, around the banquet tables of Heaven, she will be able to tell the story of a victory that glorifies God.

Whether or not Tom responds, real territory in Mary's soul has been recaptured for the purposes of the Father. Those purposes are being brought about through the new freedom in Mary's life. A pocket of numbness and rebellion has been cleaned out and is, for the first time, available to the Lord for His unfettered purposes. Her passion to love her husband with the truth is now unleashed. For the first time, she is truly his "helpmeet," a term that has been trivialized by making it synonymous with "domestic helper." In reality, the helpmeet is primarily to help her husband with his *character*.

Mary's story at the banquet tables will revolve around her adventure in becoming, for the first time, a real helper to her husband. She will know great joy in telling of how she loved and respected her husband enough to be truthful with him in love. And she will marvel at the breathtaking freedom God permitted her as she walked the dizzy heights of loving well.

CHAPTER FIFTEEN

What Is the Conscience *For?*

IT WOULD BE TERRIBLY wrong to conclude from all the preceding that the conscience is in itself a bad thing. God invented the conscience; it is His gift to us. While the conscience is often misused (as is sex, another of God's inventions), we shouldn't handle its misuse by ignoring it. Our conscience has a wonderful function: *It labors to develop and sanctify the good gift of our humanness by leading us to God.* Conscience, then, is a spur for directing our humanity closer and closer to what it was built for: relationship with God. It works to alert us when we have strayed from the path of developing intimacy with the Father.

There is something crucial here. Our conscience is to alert us that we have strayed from the direction our humanity was designed to go: toward relationship with God. Please note: The conscience is there to alert us to transgression, not to convict us that our very existence is a transgression. The whole idea behind the biblical concept of conscience is that it is good that we exist, because in existing we have opportunity to bear witness to God by keeping a clear conscience under His divine authority (see 1 Peter 2:19). This sinful world, with all its disappointments and its mockery of our longings, tempts us to pursue a perversion of humanity: a self-sufficient commitment to create a haven on earth, no matter how much we have to ignore God and violate people to do so. On the other hand, God calls us to seek haven in Him (by loving Him with all our heart, soul, mind, and strength) and to *be* a haven to others by loving them well.

The conscience, then, is there to alert us to this *perversion* of humanity. It does *not* function to condemn our humanity itself. Being human is not our problem. Our problem lies in being *sinful*. Our sinfulness with its anxious self-assertion drives us to pervert our humanity by steering it toward self-sufficiency rather than toward love for God and others. The healthy conscience exposes and condemns perversion (in this broad sense as well as in the narrow sense), but the condemnation is intended to reconcile us to God. Conscience can be a doorway to God. It does not hold our very humanity at arm's length in disgust but labors to sanctify and develop our humanity by leading us to God.

The guilt-driven conscience, on the other hand, makes no distinction between humanness and its perversion. It condemns us for being human, for existing at all. This is because it operates out of a shame-based past. As we have already seen, when shame is applied to our God-given dignity (father-to-child: "you're a pest"; child-to-self: "I am shameful for wanting to play with my dad"), it is like acid on a tender wound. Dignity withers and is kept bound up by the continued application of shame. But now the shame is internalized and applied *by* the self *to* the self. In other words, we take on the job of shaming ourselves, even when those who shamed us have mellowed, died, or changed their tactics.

As shame becomes more and more a way of life, we feel progressively more guilt about our very existence. It is shameful that we darken the face of the earth with our presence. The overactive conscience develops as a way of apologizing for the "sin" of being here. Further, it acts to "earn" permission for staying here through the avenue of impeccable performance.

The Bible, however, *never condemns us for being human.* It does condemn us for perverting our humanity. It condemns us for taking the gift of humanness and using it to carve out a personal comfort zone built on fear and selfishness. Whenever we defend that comfort zone, we are asserting that God is a poor haven and that we must see to our own safety. It is then that we deserve the condemnation of conscience. It is then that we become a perversion of humanness.

When we use our human capacities in a perverted way, pitting our humanness against the God who created it, the job of conscience is to bring judgment and blame on us in an effort to persuade us of our folly. And our folly runs deep. Proverbs 19:3 is a sobering verse in this regard: "The foolishness of man subverts his way, and his heart rages against the LORD." Our foolishness undermines us, yet we don't see it happening. Our foolishness is subtle, or better said, we make it subtle by deceiving ourselves about it.

God gives us the gift of conscience to alert us to our true foolishness, but the falsely guilt-driven conscience completely ruins our chances of clearly seeing that foolishness. The overactive conscience acts as if it is convicting us of the sin of foolishness when, in reality, it is convicting us of the "sin" of being human. Working hard to atone for being human is inherently foolish. And it blinds us to the real foolishness in our souls, that of working to create a haven, apart from God, in a sinful, fallen world.

Here, we need to return to the parable of the Pharisee and the tax gatherer who went to the temple to pray (Luke 18:9-14). Richard Crashaw, an English religious poet, penned the following lines on this parable:

Two went to pray? O, rather say
One went to brag, the other to pray;
One stands up close and treads on high,
Where the other dares not lend his eye;
One nearer to the altar trod,
The other to the altar's God.[1]

Crashaw's poem illustrates nicely that the guilt-driven conscience has missed the point entirely. The Pharisee is oriented toward the altar, that is, to a defensive, self-protective display of the trappings of righteousness. The tax gatherer, by contrast, knows that he has nothing to offer, not even the trappings of piety. He throws himself on the character of God, saying, "God be merciful to me, the sinner" (18:13).

In essence, the tax gatherer comes to God naked. He is not protected by his own merit; he is stripped of bargaining power. The Pharisee, on the other hand, moves through the parable pointing smugly at his fig leaves: "See, God, I'm covered by this and that." It makes no difference that the "fig leaves" have religious overtones, the Pharisee is still operating out of self-sufficiency. At the heart of this attitude is deep cynicism about the character of God. The Pharisee's actions reveal that he sees God as too small to be merciful but just petty enough to be bargained with.

In this, the Pharisee is like Adam and Eve in Genesis 3:7-13. There, the first humans, in the awareness of sin, emit an absolute cloud of lying, blaming, rationalizing, and protesting in order to remove the spotlight of God's judgment. Like the Pharisee, they have become self-sufficient. Rather than casting themselves nakedly on the character of God, they seek to obscure His vision by twisting the truth and blaming Him and each other. How different it might have been had they not fled from God. How different if they had knelt before Him, saying, "Father, we have sinned. We come to You knowing our penalty and

hoping for Your mercy. We trust You to decide our future."
How different if they had said, "God be merciful to me, the
sinner."

The Pharisee emits a cloud of self-sufficient piety.
Adam and Eve emit a cloud of self-sufficient scrambling.
Both are distorting the truth because of their deep cynicism about the character of God. The tax gatherer has
it right. He knows that all he really can trust, knowing his fallen state in a fallen world, is the character
of God.

The task of the conscience is to direct us to the character of God when we have strayed from trusting Him in
any way. Sometimes, our lack of trust is obvious. We
curse, lie, cheat, commit adultery, and so forth. At other
times, our lack of trust is quite subtle, buried in attitudes like self-contempt, other-centered contempt, fear
of rejection or in behaviors like overeating, possessive-
ness toward our friends, compulsive television-watching,
or over-busyness. At the core of such attitudes or behaviors is some level of doubt regarding God's character.

Our conscience, then, is part of an arsenal that God
uses to prick our awareness, to stir us from our "waking
sleep" to *see* our self-sufficiency and our doubts about
God's character and to help us work through and turn
from both.

One of the biggest obstacles to our growth as believers is our lack of awareness. We really do not contem-
plate life and the real significance either of things outside us—events and relationships—or of things inside
us—moods, attitudes, memories, subtly held goals, and
feelings. We numb ourselves to the real impact of these
things, preferring to live unfeelingly beneath an avalanche
of overcommitment, television, compulsive relational and
behavioral patterns, workaholism, denial, and distorted
thinking.

Consider the idea of a compulsive behavioral pattern,

for instance. Several months ago, I found myself holding open the refrigerator door, staring somewhat blankly,
hoping a small but delicious snack would jump out at me.
At first, I didn't realize what I was doing. It would have
been quite possible for me to survey the contents of the
refrigerator, find the least unappealing food there, and
mindlessly consume it, chewing in the preoccupied way
that a cow does.

Fortunately, I "came to" in front of the refrigerator and
asked myself, "What am I doing?" And then, "Am I really
hungry?" The answer was no. So what *was* I doing? I
began to survey my feelings instead of the refrigerator.
I slowly became aware of disappointment gnawing at my
insides. What was I disappointed about? My mind worked
its way back through the recent past. Before long, I arrived
at the real issue. About a half-hour before, I had opened
a letter from the only university anywhere near me that
offered an accredited doctorate in a field I badly wanted to
pursue. The gist of the letter was that this program did not
accept part-time students. Since part-time status was my
only hope of working through this program, I was deeply
frustrated and disappointed by this news. But I didn't
realize how frustrated I was until I found myself staring
into the refrigerator vaguely hoping for comfort.

It would have been so easy for me to have followed this
pattern: find a snack, eat it, feel a bit better, struggle with
the remaining repressed disappointment, hit the refrigerator again, feel a bit better, and so on. The sensation
of food warmly filling my stomach would be functioning
as a substitute for the comfort I needed from God. At the
heart of my urge to eat, then, was the hope of finding a
substitute for God. Why? Because I do not trust Him to
touch the ache I feel inside.

Here is where my conscience needs to warn me: "You
are moving away from the One who loves you and seeking to replace Him with a sensation that won't last." But

before my conscience can bring this level of warning, it must be allowed to warn me on a prior level: "It is wrong for you to keep yourself unaware of what is really going on inside you." But how can my conscience function, even on this prior level, if I am numbing my soul with the compulsive consumption of food?

Conscience, then, is a voice of awareness to which I need desperately to listen. How can I hear it? There are two essentials: (1) I must repent of my false conscience, my overactive conscience (the four previous chapters were concerned with developing this repentance); and (2) I must stop and explore the unexplored, examining my behavior for hidden functions.

For example, Leah was a woman who struggled with homosexuality. It wasn't hard to see that counseling had to include discovering and working through the purpose or function of the homosexuality. What was less obvious was discovering the function of more "trivial" but still compulsive behaviors. One of them was her habit of getting on the phone to check up on her friends. She would see if they were awake in the morning, whether they had gotten back from a trip safely, whether they had had a good weekend, and so forth. Many of these were long-distance calls. The calls were compulsive, frequent, and were clearly not about the supposed purpose of the call.

During one session, Leah reported calling a friend a thousand miles away that morning to see if she had awakened on time. I confronted her on the inappropriateness of the call. After some defensive responses to me, she was able to admit that the calls (and some other behavior patterns) sprang from a need to be in such consistent, close contact with others that she actually felt she was "in their skin." She needed to feel that she was merged with others, that she lived through them, so complete was their fusing. By over-identifying with others, she could avoid the dread she felt at standing alone, at being a whole person without needing the prop of living through others. The role of homosexuality in helping her feel fused with someone else became painfully obvious.

Not everyone struggles with homosexuality, but everyone does struggle with behavior that saps awareness (like standing in front of the refrigerator looking for cud to chew). I recall another counselee, Linda, who looked away every time I raised my coffee cup to my lips. After realizing what she was doing, I asked, "Is my drinking this distasteful to you?" She replied that it was. I asked why. She thought for a bit and began to unravel a painful tale about sitting in the parking lot of a police station while her aunt went inside to post bond for her mother who had been arrested for drunk driving. Linda was afraid and embarrassed by her mother's actions. She was six years old.

While waiting for her aunt and mother to return, she happened to notice a house across the street where the kitchen window was open. An obese woman with disheveled hair, wearing a dirty robe, walked through the kitchen, opened the refrigerator, and drank greedily from a milk carton. She wiped her mouth on her sleeve, turned, and slouched out of view. All of Linda's disgust was transferred onto that woman and focused especially on her graceless act of drinking. It was safer to be repulsed by that woman than by her own mother.

Thirty years later, she was beginning to get in touch with that revulsion, all because she had looked away several times while I was drinking coffee. The emphasis here should not be on feeling that we need to go over our behavior with a fine-toothed comb. Rather, we should concentrate on seeing how creative and consistent we are with keeping awareness at bay.

The conscience is there to warn us, to increase our awareness of how we may be failing to love God fully and to love our neighbor deeply. The greater our commitment to ward off awareness, the more our conscience will be crippled. And the more it is crippled, the more likely it is to develop into a false conscience, a guilt-driven conscience.

Here, then, is an important distinction between a healthy conscience and an overactive one: The latter always works to keep our awareness limited to the fact that we are flaws as human beings. On the other hand, the healthy conscience increases our awareness of straying from the path of loving God and people. But the purpose is not to bring final condemnation (Romans 8:1). Healthy guilt is a prelude to grace, not self-contempt. When our conscience places us in the spotlight of judgment, it is not to pronounce a sentence against us; rather, it is to point us in a new direction, showing us an alternative to continuing our transgression. It shows us the way of repentance, the way of joyously changing the direction of our life. Our life now takes the direction, more and more, of deeply loving God and people.

Our conscience, then, is like a liberty bell. When it rings, we should be both alarmed and excited. We should be alarmed that we have strayed from the path of loving God and people. We should be excited about the opportunity to repent and return from subhumanness to the humanness that freely loves. We should be alarmed that our awareness has temporarily narrowed to an obsessive focus on *getting* from others and from God. We should be deliriously excited that our vision can expand again to see the big picture: Life lies in loving God and people and in thus being a city set on a hill. The Light that comes from that city reflects the freedom to love that emerges from a conscience that liberates rather than confines.

Chapter Four—False Guilt Is the *Source* of an Overactive Conscience
1. Walker Percy, *The Second Coming* (New York: Pocket Books, 1981), page 5.

Chapter Seven—The Foolish Heart Maneuvers for Independence
1. Nathaniel Hawthorne, *The Scarlet Letter* (Topeka, KS: Econo-Clad Books, 1987), page 141.

Chapter Nine—False Guilt as a Subtle Critique of God
1. I owe the idea of being marooned and finding a message in a bottle to Walker Percy, *The Message in the Bottle* (New York: The Noonday Press, 1975), pages 119-149.
2. At this point, many sit back down and say, "This is too good to be true. This is a fairy tale. Next thing you know, I'll be believing in Santa Claus." Others sit down and say, "I've been all over this island looking for a way out. I didn't find any boat. Who knows who wrote this stupid message, anyway? Maybe the last

guy who died here wrote it to torment the next guy or to give him the illusion of hope. Well, it didn't work." The people who say these kinds of things and who never check to see if the message is true are called unbelievers.

Chapter Eleven—Embracing Christ's Atonement Rather Than Our Own

1. Brent Curtis, *Guilt*, IBC Discussion Guides Series (Colorado Springs, CO: NavPress, 1992), page 19.
2. Dan Allender, *Bold Love* (Colorado Springs, CO: NavPress, 1992), page 81.

Chapter Twelve—Moving Away from an Overactive Conscience by Cultivating Thankfulness

1. Flannery O'Connor, *The Complete Stories* (New York: Farrar, Straus, Giroux, 1990), pages 269-70.
2. Alan Jones, *Soulmaking* (New York: Harper-Collins, 1989), page 192.
3. Irvin Yalom, *Existential Psychotherapy* (New York: Basic Books, 1980), page 196.
4. I. Howard Marshall, *Commentary on Luke*, New International Greek Testament Commentaries (Grand Rapids, MI: Eerdmans, 1978), page 208. See also Luke 4:1 for this idea of fullness meaning "completely."
5. Jones, page 176.

Chapter Thirteen—Moving Away from an Overactive Conscience By Cultivating Freedom

1. Walker Percy, *Lost in the Cosmos* (New York: Farrar, Straus, Giroux, 1983), page 76.
2. Percy, page 77.
3. Percy, pages 78-79.
4. Irvin Yalom, *Existential Psychotherapy* (New York: Basic Books, 1980), pages 46-47.

Chapter Fourteen—A Portrait of Freedom

1. I. Howard Marshall, *Commentary on Luke*, New International Greek Testament Commentaries (Grand Rapids, MI: Eerdmans, 1978), page 311.

Chapter Fifteen—What Is the Conscience *For?*

1. William Cullen Bryant, ed., *Library of World Poetry* (New York: Avenel Books, 1970), page 259.

A U T H O R
▼ ▼

Steve Shores is currently director of the Center for Biblical Counseling of Hickory (North Carolina). After four years as director of counseling services and assistant professor of pastoral ministries at Dallas Theological Seminary, Steve got tired of the big city and moved to Hickory to set up a private practice in counseling. The skyline of Hickory (mostly trees) is much more conducive to raising a family.

Steve is married to Susan, and they have three daughters: Katy, Jenny, and Christy. This is Steve's biggest arena of education. It is informal but rigorous.

As for formal education, Steve holds master's degrees from Dallas Theological Seminary in theology and Grace Theological Seminary in biblical counseling. He is one of the cofounders of Biblical Counseling Ministries and its seminar entitled "Taking a Clear Look." He has also published a discussion guide entitled *Stress* with NavPress in the Institute of Biblical Counseling Series.

A C K N O W L E D G M E N T S

▼ ▼

The speaker at a recent marriage seminar asked, "How many men in the room have a true mentor?" He had defined a mentor as a man walking ahead of you on the path toward God. Every so often, he looks back, makes eye-contact, and says, "It can be done. Keep walking. I believe in you." I was able to raise my hand.

I smiled because the speaker and my mentor were the same man, Larry Crabb. Though we don't have a lot of contact, I see the path he walks. And he says to me, "It can be done. Don't quit. I believe in you." This book exists because I have been loved well. Only love could have awakened the books inside me. Larry has been a big part of the awakening.

So has Dan Allender. In many ways, Larry and Dan couldn't be more different. Larry's words to me have, at time, exploded like dynamite. Dan, on the other hand, sends words cutting like surgical tools. Dan loosened the cancer of syrupy-sweet passivity that had been smothering the aliveness in my soul.

Then there is Susan, my wife, to whom I dedicate this book. Susan is nuclear. Her courage to offer me the white-hot aliveness in her soul has melted my heart. No one other than Christ has cared about me so deeply as to die for me. Susan has died to many things: the lure of emotional safely and comfort, the security of distorting hard truth, the temptation to bury longing for love. Her integrity staggers me. Susan, your offer of unfading beauty stamps this book—and me—from beginning to end. It is a testament to God's work in your beautiful, yet trembling, soul.